I0822074

Maya Caciques in Early National Yucatán

A book in the Latin American and Caribbean
Arts and Culture publication initiative.
Latin American and Caribbean Arts and Culture is
supported by the Andrew W. Mellon Foundation.

Maya Caciques in Early National Yucatán

Rajeshwari Dutt

University of Oklahoma Press : Norman

Parts of chapter 4 were previously published in Rajeshwari Dutt, "Crossing Over: Caciques, Indigenous Politics and the Vecino World in Caste War Yucatán," *Ethnohistory* 61, no. 4 (2014). Reprinted with permission of Duke University Press.

Library of Congress Cataloging-in-Publication Data

Name: Dutt, Rajeshwari, 1981– author.
Title: Maya caciques in early national Yucatán / Rajeshwari Dutt.
Description: Norman : University of Oklahoma Press, 2017. | Includes bibliographical references and index.
Identifiers: LCCN 2016033836 | ISBN 978-0-8061-5578-4 (hardcover : alk. paper)
Subjects: LCSH: Mayas—Mexico—Yucatán (State)—Politics and government—19th century. | Caciques (Indian leaders)—Mexico—Yucatán (State)—History—19th century. | Mayas—Mexico—Yucatán (State)—Social conditions—19th century.
Classification: LCC F1435.3.P7 D88 2017 | DDC 305.897/427—dc23
LC record available at https//lccn.loc.gov/2016033836

The paper in this book meets the guidelines for permanence and durability of the Committee on Production Guidelines for Book Longevity of the Council on Library Resources, Inc. ∞

1 2 3 4 5 6 7 8 9 10

In memory of my father, Ashish Kumar Dasgupta
For my mother, Purabi Dasgupta

Contents

Maps

Acknowledgments

Every book has its history. Mine is one that is punctuated at every turn with incredible support from various individuals and institutions.

As a Bengali from Kolkata, India, I encountered the history of Latin America for the first time as an undergraduate in Franklin and Marshall College, located in the scenic Amish country of Pennsylvania. There amid an idyllic campus setting I benefited from the knowledge and able guidance of Eric Zolov, Leo Garofalo, Louise L. Stevenson, Doug Anthony, Joshua Goldstein, and Antonio Callari, all of whom pushed me beyond my comfort zone. Eric Zolov continues to be a wonderful friend and guide, and this book has benefited from his wisdom.

My interest in Maya history and culture began as a graduate student at Carnegie Mellon University in Pittsburgh. I was fortunate in having Paul Eiss as my thesis advisor. With his profound knowledge of both Maya history and anthropology, Paul encouraged my interests in Maya caciques and offered support and criticism at just the right moments. As I began the laborious process of writing the book, Paul provided an excellent sounding board for my ideas and support in moments of despair. There are literally no words to express my gratitude to him.

In Pittsburgh, several other scholars provided invaluable support and guidance. Conversations with Roger Rouse—over steaming cups of coffee—often opened my eyes to fresh perspectives from which to review my work on caciques. John Soluri, Rick Maddox, and Kate

Lynch gave unstinting advice and were voices of wisdom as I navigated the often-unsteady waters of academic research.

I also gratefully acknowledge the support of the History Department of CMU for funding that enabled me to conduct research at the archives in Mérida, Yucatán.

My research in Yucatán was made possible through the unwavering support of the archive staff of the Archivo General del Estado de Yucatán in Mérida. I would like especially to acknowledge the support given by Piedad Peniche Rivero (Suzie Peniche), former director of the archive. I am also indebted to Armando Chi Estrella, Karla Caballero Negron, Cinthia Vanessa Fernández Vergara, Lizbeth García Torres, and other archive staff for their generosity and support. I would also like to thank the staff at the Centro de Apoyo a la Investigación Histórica de Yucatán in Mérida for their help during my research.

Writing a book is never easy. It is harder still to do so when you are living oceans away from your research site. Nevertheless, the Indian Institute of Technology Mandi located in Kamand, India, has provided a conducive environment for immersing myself in my research and writing. Generous professional development grants from the Institute have made it possible for me to make archival visits to Yucatán. I am grateful to the director, Timothy Gonsalves, for supporting my interests in Latin American and Maya history.

I am grateful to the circle of scholars of Yucatán for their support at various times. I have benefited immensely from being included in the Yucatán in Pennsylvania Roundtables. In particular, I am grateful to Matthew Restall for his support and encouragement. I am also grateful to Peter Leventhal, Amara Solari, Spencer Delbridge, and Crista Cesario, who as part of the Roundtables provided me with feedback on my work. Thanks are also due to Heather McCrea for sharing her work on Yucatán with me.

Every writer longs for the perfect editor. Thomas Krause of the University of Oklahoma Press has been the most encouraging and supportive editor and has guided me superbly from the very beginning. Without his excellent feedback and knowledge as an editor, this book would not be. I am thankful to my manuscript editor Emily Schuster and to my copyeditor John Thomas. Their keen eyes and minute attention to details improved the manuscript considerably. I am also grateful to the anonymous reviewers of the book manuscript for their insightful comments, which have greatly improved this book. Thanks are also due to Bill Nelson, who is responsible for the cartography in this book, and to Amron Gravett, who made the index. I am also grateful to the Mellon Foundation's Latin American and Caribbean Arts and Culture initiative, which funded the indexing, cartography, and related expenses of the book.

Friends matter a great deal. They matter even more when you need to counterbalance the solitude of research and writing. My college roommate Amanda Williamson continues to be a source of joy and laughter. At CMU, I benefited from several friends and colleagues: Yan Gao, Ashwin Kumar, Patrick Zimmerman, Fidel Makoto Campet, Lee Jared Vinsel, Jessica Barber Klanderud, Sonya Barclay, John Weigel, and Oana Suditu. At IIT, Mandi, Ramna Thakur and Reshma Sao have provided friendship and support. In Mérida, Indira Ceballos Barrera and her family gave me a home away from home.

More than any other, it is to my family that I am grateful for putting up with my seemingly unending research. I owe my interest in life stories to my grandmother, Aruna Dasgupta. To my father, Ashish Kumar Dasgupta, I am grateful for all his sacrifices that enabled me to pursue my dreams. My mother, Purabi Dasgupta, continues to be a source of strength and inspiration. Thanks are also due to my brother Nataraj Dasgupta for his support. I thank my parents-in-law, Vijay Kumar Dutt and Poonam Dutt, for their unstinting support. My husband, Varun Dutt, has been with me from the first moment I took an interest in Maya history till the ink dried on the book manuscript. To him I give my heartfelt thanks for his endless patience, love, and understanding. We welcomed our daughter Virangana into this world while I was in the process of writing this book. My final thanks are to her for her infectious laughter and mischievous ways. She reminds me every day that the greatest joys often lie in the smallest things.

Maya Caciques in Early National Yucatán

Nineteenth-century Yucatán. Map by Bill Nelson. Copyright © 2017, University of Oklahoma Press.

Introduction

Andrés Canché succeeded to the post of cacique (indigenous leader) of Cenotillo in January 1834 under inauspicious circumstances. A cholera epidemic had decimated the local population in the previous year, including the then cacique. Now, it fell on Canché to provide leadership and representation to the indigenous residents of the embattled town. Over the next thirty years Canché would navigate the challenges of being a cacique in early national Yucatán. Major political shifts would take place at the national and regional levels during this period, but Canché, like other caciques, would experience them in extremely local and personal ways. By the time of his final retirement from the office in 1864, Canché would be an expert politician in his own right—one who had made powerful local alliances while defending the interests of his indigenous community. At the same time, Canché would retire from office a weary man facing poverty and sickness. More than a biographical sketch, Canché's life can be used as a window into understanding how indigenous caciques negotiated the early years of post-independence Yucatán.

In 1972, when the doyen of Latin American history, James Lockhart, retold the story of the Spanish conquest through biographical sketches of individual conquistadores, he unlocked for later historians of Latin America the power of a life story.[1] *Maya Caciques in Early National Yucatán* is set in Mexico's Yucatán region in the Maya heartland in the years of change that spanned the early decades of post-independence Mexico. In it individual life stories of Maya caciques become the fulcrum around which questions of power and change are evoked and debated.

THE SMALL PICTURE

The Maya of Yucatán proved notoriously difficult to conquer. In fact, whereas the Spanish conquistadores took two years to defeat the great Aztec empire, this other Mesoamerican civilization held out for almost twenty years. Even then the Maya empire contained pockets beyond the pale of Spanish control. By the time the city of Mérida was founded in 1542, Yucatán had witnessed three distinct phases of conquest expeditions. It was probably the lack of a centralized structure of power prominent in empires such as the Aztecs' that ensured Maya survival—that and the comparative unattractiveness of the peninsula, which was singularly lacking in precious metals that were so important to the Spanish.

Located in the southeast of Mexico, Yucatán remained a Spanish colonial backwater, creating the conditions for a unique historical trajectory. The relative lack of incentive to settle down in Yucatán meant that the Spanish chose to rely heavily on preexisting Maya social and political hierarchies to administer the region. The precolonial figure of the *batab* (pl. *batabob*), or Maya headman, became the vital linchpin around which the old and the new achieved a marriage of convenience. Under the Spanish, the batab became the cacique, a crucial intermediary between indigenous communities and the Spanish government.

Our story is about the batab or, rather, the batab-turned-cacique. Although the early conquerors, intent on spending as little energy as possible on Yucatán, left the cacique very much to his own devices, by the late colonial period the world of the cacique was beginning to change. Beset with its own internal problems, the Spanish colonial state began streamlining administration in what are now known as the Bourbon reforms. These left an indelible mark on local communities. In Yucatán they meant the introduction of government officials for the first time into areas previously left largely to be administered by caciques. The progressive proscription of cacique power continued into the early decades after independence (1821), with the new liberal state plucking out one feather of privilege after another, leaving the cacique bare and relatively powerless.

There are two ways to tell this story. One is to look at the big picture. Here the story is an obvious one. The cacique becomes powerless and declines over time. In fact this is easily borne out by the fact that the office of cacique was finally abolished in Yucatán by 1869. And this story would have merit. After all, that is how much of the history of indigenous people in Latin America has been told: after an illustrious if savage past, indigenous people succumbed to colonialism and over the course of the eighteenth and nineteenth centuries declined, albeit with minor fits of resistance.

And then there is another way to tell the story—by looking at the small picture, the micro-history. This is the story we unravel when we examine the lives of individual caciques in the towns and villages of Yucatán. In this retelling the story is not of failure and decline but rather one of survival, even empowerment. Here we find individuals who overcome exclusionary state policies through strategic local alliances, who use their personal relationships to transcend barriers to political power. *Maya Caciques in Early National Yucatán* is the indigenous history of the nineteenth century retold from the vantage point of embattled intermediaries. It is a reminder that the "big picture" in fact often resides in the smallest spaces.

CLIENTELISM AS A HISTORICAL PHENOMENON

"You are an Indian from India studying Indians in Latin America. I am sure there is a joke in there somewhere." This is what a professor I met at a conference in the United States once remarked when he learned I was working on the Maya. Jokes aside, living and working in the two regions I have been struck by how the flavor of local rural politics appears to transcend national boundaries.

In villages in India the state is most often experienced through encounters with local officials. The state here does not exist as something external to or outside of civil society. Collapsing Western distinctions between "state" and "civil society," anthropologist Akhil

Gupta working in North India has shown that boundaries between the two become blurred at the local level when local officials representing the state interact with people on the ground. Gupta writes: "At the local level it becomes difficult to experience the state as an ontologically coherent entity: what one confronts instead is much more discrete and fragmentary—land records officials, village development workers, the Electricity Board, headmen, the police, and the Block Development Office."[2] In the Indian village the local Sarpanch forms an intermediary figure between the government and the community. The Sarpanch is the elected head of the village governing body and is vested with the task of overseeing government programs in the village. Villagers approach him for various needs, and he can augment his power through links to local officials such as the local MLA (member of the legislative assembly) or the BDO (block development officer).[3] In these villages the state has a penumbral quality, ubiquitous yet visible only as a pale shadow foregrounded by local officials. Sifting through documents in the archives in Mérida, Yucatán, miles away from India, I had a sense of déjà vu.

We often regard the clientelism rife in rural areas of developing nations as somehow timeless. What could be more natural, more obvious than that members of face-to-face communities should have personal relationships from which they derive mutual benefit? It is no wonder that, whereas the studies of formal institutions of power such as the state are overproduced and overmarketed, there is comparatively little attention paid to understanding the historical substrates of informal power. In fact, we think of phenomena such as clientelism and favoritism as so much a part of human nature that we fail to consider that these behaviors could have a historical dimension.

The word "cacique" is used a lot in Mexico. In an archive where I once worked, the supervisor was often referred to by the archive staff as a "cacica," with all the connotations of power, favoritism, even despotism that the word implies. Though the revolutionary caciques of twentieth-century Mexico perhaps signify the quintessential cacique in the popular mind, caciques as historical figures have existed in Latin America since the sixteenth century. Spanish conquistadores coined the term from the Arawak language and applied it indiscriminately to refer to indigenous headmen across Spanish America.

Over time the cacique became a stock figure—an intermediary or middleman walking the tightrope between the state on the one hand and the community on the other. Amid all the stereotyping, the historical process that made a cacique act as a cacique gets lost.

In *Maya Caciques in Early National Yucatán*, I examine the Maya cacique during the late colonial and early national period in Yucatán. Yet this book is about much more than the fate of caciques in nineteenth-century Yucatán. It reveals a much bigger story about the emergence, evolution, and normalization of particular forms of political conduct in the decades following independence. I show that what we consider to be a generic, obvious, or "natural" phenomenon—clientelism—has a specific history that can be illuminated by a study of Yucatán's caciques. The fact that the cacique behaved like a cacique was not something natural or inevitable. Rather, the behaviors we associate with these figures arose out of a set of historical circumstances and conjunctures. If caciques represent a form of informal power, then this book breaks down the assumption that informal power exists in any timeless way. Rather, it has as long and complicated a history as institutions of formal power such as the state.

This book is also fundamentally about state re-formation. It adds to the growing body of literature in Latin American history that views state formation not as a top-down process but as something that is experienced and negotiated at a local level by indigenous and subaltern populations.[4] In the process, the study engages the lively theoretical debate on the nature of state-community interaction. Tim Mitchell coined the term "state effect" to explain the way the state appears to be outside of or external to the civil society.[5] In reality, as Gupta has shown, boundaries between state and society become blurred at the local level when local officials representing the state interact with people on the ground. My research builds on his insights by showing how the state's presence was felt and negotiated by caciques in everyday interactions with government functionaries.

As Maya caciques fashioned a new form of political conduct, they fundamentally reshaped forms of local governance instituted by the state. With the hand of the state reaching farther and farther in after independence, the value systems of villages seemed to be tearing at the seams. With their old privileges dying out, more than ever caciques needed to legitimize themselves through their association with what was now held as the most sacred, the most powerful: the state. Paul Friedrich's observation of caciques of twentieth-century Mexico holds true for Maya caciques of the nineteenth century as well: "The agrarian cacique has always conspicuously attempted to validate his power by appeals to higher political and governmental levels of leaders, institutions and ideas."[6] As caciques sought to achieve this through informal clientelist relationships, they reinserted themselves into governance in ways that had never been envisioned by the state.

The office of the cacique evolved out of the needs of the Spanish crown to administer conquered territories effectively. Particularly in areas such as Yucatán where there was no real economic incentive for the early conquistadores to settle and where the local language and culture presented a real barrier to Spanish administration, the separate *república* system proved to be a viable option for indirect control. Under this system, the colonial society was divided into two components: the *república de indios* and the *república de españoles*, under which indigenous and Spanish worlds, respectively, were supposed to remain separate. Each indigenous community was governed by a república or *cabildo* (council) comprising indigenous officers and headed by the indigenous headman, or cacique. Accordingly, the survival of the cacique was tied to the fate of the república system. In Yucatán, the pre-Columbian figure of the Maya indigenous headman, or batab, became coopted by the Spanish conquerors, and the república was grafted onto the pre-Conquest Maya geopolitical setup of the *cah*, or community. In Yucatán the office of the batab and the cacique merged, with the two titles used interchangeably.

The sixteenth and seventeenth centuries did not witness a sea change on this point; caciques continued to behave very much as the batabob of yore. Because of the marginal position of Yucatán within the colony, in the early colonial period the Maya enjoyed a high degree of autonomy, with Maya chiefs retaining many of their traditional powers and privileges. Maya caciques continued to organize feasts, arbitrate justice, and govern the internal workings of indigenous communities. The main political alliances and disputes at this time remained mainly confined within elite Maya society.

The first palpable changes occurred in the late colonial period with the implementation of Bourbon reforms. With the aim of streamlining administration, the colonial government began to station its own officials in regional headquarters. Even at this point, however, Maya caciques continued to be seen as vital intermediaries by the colonial government, and effective control of the locality still remained in their hands. Some caciques did build interdependent relations with government functionaries, but these were not systematically converted into identifiable long-term alliances.

The emergence of liberalism as an ideology of governance in the early nineteenth century marked the beginning of the decline in the official role of the indigenous república. For liberal reformers the separate república system contradicted the ideals of equality of all citizens. Moreover, for modernizing elite the república system legitimized economic practices (e.g., indigenous communal property rights) that were anathema to liberal economic ideals, which centered on private property and the sanctity of the unfettered market.

The liberal onslaught on indigenous autonomy began with the Constitution of Cádiz, whereby the indigenous repúblicas were abolished for a brief period (1813–14). They were brought back with the restoration of monarchy and then again abolished in 1820. After independence the system was restored again in 1824, mainly driven by problems of collecting taxes. The restored república and cacique now were stripped of all their former functions under colonialism with the exception of collecting taxes and keeping their communities in line with the needs of the government (e.g., through recruitment of labor). Instead, as a result of municipalization town councils (*ayuntamientos*) with attendant nonindigenous officials were brought into being, effectively challenging the power of caciques in localities. The liberal constitution of Yucatán of 1841 in effect abolished the república for a third time simply by not mentioning it. Then, the república was brought back for a final time in 1847 with the outbreak of the violent Caste War—arguably the longest and bloodiest rebellion in Latin American history. In the 1860s, Yucatán experienced a new experiment with government, a French intervention that foisted a monarch on Mexico. Surprisingly, repúblicas proved to be important bodies during the brief rule of Emperor Maximilian, who tried to appease the Maya peasantry. A couple of years after the restoration of a federal republic, indigenous repúblicas were abolished once and for all on January 1, 1869.[7]

After 1821 the incursion of the state into localities through the newly established ayuntamientos gradually stripped Maya caciques of their privileges, with nonindigenous officials such as *alcaldes, jueces de paz, jefes políticos*, and *subdelegados* eventually usurping authority in localities. This institution of ayuntamientos constituted no less than a municipal revolution. And this revolution colored every nook and cranny of provincial life in post-independence Yucatán. The changes wrought by the incursion of government officials in areas previously left almost solely in the hands of caciques would have important repercussions, not just in terms of governance but also in the very manner in which politics was now conducted at the local level.

Document after document from this period returns the same picture of increasing cacique dependence on government officials. Every document also adds to our picture of the emergence of a clientelist politics that over time became solidified as the modus operandi of village politics. But the clientelist politics that caciques increasingly engaged in and which began to characterize cacique politics by the mid-nineteenth century did not emerge overnight; nor was it inevitable. Current scholarship of indigenous history notes the gradual decline of indigenous power over the eighteenth and nineteenth centuries as well as the mediating role played by the cacique. Using the method of micro-history, however, this book revises this assumption by showing how indigenous caciques, stripped by the state of traditional power and the right to administer their communities, were able to insert themselves back into the process of governance through strategic local alliances.

Rather than gradually losing the preceding kinds of power or access to them, as is generally characterized in the literature, caciques began to fashion a new political repertoire, forming clearly identifiable alliances with new local officials. Caciques have been characterized over and over again as "intermediaries." I qualify this assumption by emphatically positing that the nature of caciques' mediation was first and foremost a political one. Interestingly, the more power caciques lost as mediators in the post-independence period, the more politicized they became. The particular nature of their political conduct can be subsumed to one term: clientelism. As previous forms of political participation became more and more difficult to continue in the wake of exclusionary policies instituted by the state, caciques made clientelism the new modus operandi of local politics. Moreover, unlike the more community-based politics of the colonial period, the clientelism of the post-independence period would be of an individualistic and personal nature. The life stories in *Maya Caciques in Early National Yucatán* underline the historical trajectory that led to this transformation.

THE POLITICAL INTERMEDIARY

One of the earliest conceptualizations of caciques as mediators can be attributed to Eric Wolf. In his 1956 article "Aspects of Group Relations in a Complex Society: Mexico," Wolf posited the figure of the cultural "broker" who formed the link between Mexican peasant communities and the national state. For Wolf, "In post-Columbian Mexico, these mediating functions were first carried out by the leaders of Indian corporate communities." These caciques, or in Wolf's words "leaders of Indian corporate communities," appeared to him to be "Janus-faced," brokers who "must serve some of the interests of groups operating on both the community and the national level, and they must cope with the conflicts raised by the collision of these interests. . . . They often act as buffers between groups, maintaining the tensions which provide the dynamic of their actions."[8]

After Wolf, some of the most important scholars of Latin American history including James Lockhart and Charles Gibson characterized caciques as mediators and brokers. In *Early Latin America*, Lockhart and Stuart Schwartz described caciques as "vital intermediaries."[9] Writing about Spanish conquest in Mesoamerica, Gibson noted that caciques adopted cultural accouterments that seemed to place them between Spanish and indigenous worlds: "In time, caciques and principals became thoroughly Hispanic in material culture while they retained their status as privileged Indians."[10] Using the case of the indigenous elite of Cuernavaca, Robert Haskett underscored this duality of cacique experience and the forms of adaptation and accommodation that allowed caciques to tread on both worlds.[11] Scholars such as Gibson also depicted caciques as middlemen, helping the state in recruitment of labor and collection of tribute.[12]

Although this view of indigenous caciques as middlemen is not without merit, it also threatens to fix the position of these elite perpetually between the state and the community. The common or stock image of caciques as middlemen pervades historical literature. Overemphasis on caciques as mediators, however, tends to depoliticize these figures. There is a very real danger of viewing caciques as disinterested conduits and of seeing mediation as some form of translation.

Recent scholarship in both Latin American and Yucatecan history has challenged this image, instead portraying caciques as political agents in their own right. Greg Grandin in his study of the K'iche elite of Guatemala shows how indigenous leaders engaged in political maneuvering to retain power.[13] Sinclair Thomson in his study of La Paz suggests that, although structurally caciques may have occupied an intermediate position between the state and the community, in the eyes of the community these figures exercised vital political functions.[14] Significantly, scholars such as Yanna Yannakakis and Alida Metcalf have underscored the ways in which native intermediaries functioned not as neutral mediators but as intrinsic elements in power plays between the state and indigenous communities.[15] Contemporary scholars of Yucatán such as Terry Rugeley and Matthew Restall have successfully portrayed the political nature of the cacique. Rugeley sees the decline of official status of caciques and their subsequent leadership of rebel groups as contributing factors to the emergence of the Caste War.[16]

Maya Caciques in Early National Yucatán contributes to this conversation in three distinct ways. First, the book holds that mediation was not a simple, linear event but complex, stratified, and nonlinear. Thus, for instance, mediation did not always follow the linear continuum of patron-broker-client—the model of state-cacique-community with the cacique as the one perpetually mediating between the state and the community. In the case of Ebtún (see chapter 1), for instance, the government itself became an intermediary between caciques of the rival communities Ebtún and Cuncunul. Moreover, as new layers of authority became incorporated at the local level, dissonance among different layers could lead to contending outcomes. We see instances of this dissonance in chapters 5 and 6, with the uneasy coexistence of old and new bureaucracy under the Second Mexican Empire making for complex and contradictory outcomes. Finally, this book builds on recent scholarship in Latin American and Yucatecan historiography by stressing the fundamentally political nature of cacique mediation. It emphasizes that the cacique's function as an intermediary was first and foremost a political one. By focusing on strategic local alliances forged by caciques and charting the development of caciques as vital local political figures, I aim to problematize the notion of caciques as neutral mediators. Rather, we see how as fundamentally political agents with vested interests caciques shaped the contours of that very mediation. Indeed, if necessary caciques could and did refuse to continue as intermediaries, underscoring their own power and agency despite the broader structures that constrained them.

A NOTE ON TERMINOLOGY

Given that Spanish conquistadores who coined the term "cacique" applied it universally to refer to indigenous headman across Spanish America, using the term "batab" to refer to Maya leaders is both historically accurate and culturally specific. Yet there are strong reasons to use the term "cacique" when examining these Maya indigenous leaders, especially in the early national period. For one, these indigenous headmen refer to themselves as caciques in most extant Spanish-language documents. The only times I have seen the term "batab" in nineteenth-century documents is when the document is in Mayan. Even in those cases I fail to see a conscious self-representation of these Maya leaders as batabob, except as a term interchangeable with cacique. Indeed, in Yucatán the terms "batab" and "cacique" came to be used interchangeably starting in the colonial period. Restall points out that except for a brief period at the onset of colonial rule (for which evidence is thin) the offices of batab and cacique (or *gobernador*) were never separate.[17] Granted, the office of the batab with its historical association to the cah had an intrinsically different meaning attached to it than that of the cacique, who was after all a Spanish instrument of administration. However, over time people came to use the terms interchangeably, especially since the two offices merged.

As well, the term "cacique" is more apt to my research because of the particular relationships I explore in this book. The term "batab" stresses the historical relationship that Maya leaders had with the cah, but the main relationships I explore are those between these Maya leaders and local authority figures (e.g., state officials, military leaders, and priests). In these relationships, Maya leaders represented themselves and were seen by these authority figures as caciques—figures who were positioned between the Maya and the Hispanic worlds.

Finally, using the term "cacique" rather than "batab" is critical to the history of political engagement of these Maya leaders that this book aims to elucidate. Over the colonial period batabob would progressively lose the traditional powers they had enjoyed in the pre-Conquest era. Focusing on indigenous leaders as batabob, therefore, tends to foreground the decline and disintegration of these figures over time. On the other hand, by focusing on these figures as caciques I am able to tell a different story—one that puts on the center stage the relationship of caciques to the state and their increasing political integration and political engagement in the early national period.

CHAPTER 1

Setting the Stage

Caciques as Political Intermediaries in Colonial Ebtún

They had come a long way. They had ridden for more than a week watching that same landscape of flat earth and dry scrub appearing and then rolling by—over and over again—as though in quiet mockery of their hopes and ambitions. It had been a costly and tiring journey for the caciques of Cuncunul and Ebtún, more than two hundred miles across the Yucatán peninsula before reaching the capital city of Mérida in the early days of February 1802. Yet they had not left their troubles behind in their distant hometowns; they carried their grievances with them to be resolved by the superior official of the province, the governor and captain general, Don Valdelomar Pérez. Both caciques had brought with them *justicias* (magistrates) of their respective pueblos, and the two parties met with the *protector de indios* (an official charged with the duty of representing indigenous pueblos) outside the court of the governor in Mérida.

Despite being a government official under the Spanish crown, this particular protector, Don Agustín Crespo, was not an unbiased third party. Rather, he represented the village of Cuncunul. Even so, he tried to listen to both caciques as they discussed their dispute over a tract of land called Tontzimin, which each pueblo claimed to be rightfully theirs and accused the other of trespassing over. Finally, the indigenous authorities of Ebtún knelt down and, using only their memory and a piece of charcoal, sketched on the floor a map of their lands, showing the leaders of Cuncunul exactly which lands had been wrongly seized.

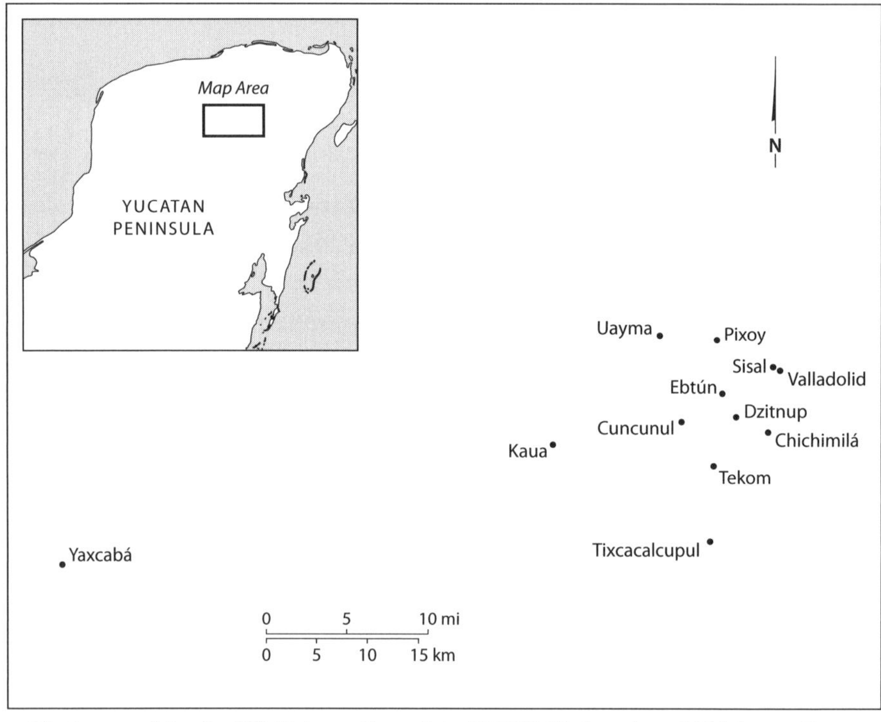

Ebtún area. Map by Bill Nelson. Copyright © 2017, University of Oklahoma Press.

As the drama unfolded, the leaders of Ebtún suggested a compromise: if the leaders of Cuncunul returned the disputed land to Ebtún, then the latter would give them twenty-five pesos. This offer reflected the Ebtún leaders' belief that in the distant past their ancestors had sold the Tontzimin land to Cuncunul for twenty-five pesos. Indeed, in hope of finally resolving this conflict, the leaders of Ebtún had brought that sum of money with them to Mérida. On this day, though, the leaders of Cuncunul were not willing to agree to this offer. They made a counteroffer: Cuncunul would pay rent for the *milpas* (cornfield) they had sown in the disputed land and remain there.

Having listened to the two caciques and their magistrates discuss this issue, Agustín Crespo asked them to gather again so that he could present them to the governor and resolve the dispute. However, the leaders of Cuncunul left, claiming that they had to get the money to give to the authorities of Ebtún for rent. In his report to the governor on 6 February 1802, the protector Agustín Crespo admitted to not knowing whether the leaders of Cuncunul would indeed return with the money. On 15 February the governor, after consulting his ministers of the exchequers and other officials, ordered the sale of Tontzimin to Ebtún by Cuncunul for twenty-five pesos and authorized a community-to-community transfer of said funds. This move to bring resolution to a dispute more than a century old would eventually fail, for Cuncunul would challenge this verdict, leading to a new spate of discussions, dissensions, and decisions from the top.

The world that Andrés Canché inherited had been in the making since at least the late eighteenth century when Spanish colonial measures to streamline administration in the Americas changed the rural political landscape. To appreciate Canché's life we must, therefore, first step back and examine this past. The journey that the caciques of Ebtún and Cuncunul undertook that February in 1802 had in reality begun in the seventeenth century and spanned almost the entire period of colonial rule in Yucatán. It is a journey whose twists and turns have survived in a collection of almost three hundred primary documents carefully transcribed and published by Ralph Roys, one of the earliest scholars of Yucatán, as *The Titles of Ebtun.*[1] The documents in this collection present an almost continuous history of a particular region (here, Ebtún and the surrounding towns of Cuncunul, Tekom, Tixcacal, and Kaua) over the course of the entire colonial period. The earliest document in the collection is from 1532, the latest, from 1829. Between these two end points, *The Titles of Ebtun* captures almost three centuries of struggle, conflict, and adaptation.[2] On the basis of these documents, the chapter offers a glimpse into cacique politics at the local level on the eve of the early national period.[3] Over the course of some thirty years starting in 1797 there were intermittent legal battles between Ebtún and Cuncunul over the Tontzimin tract, which had become part of Cuncunul's communal property since 1725. An examination of the struggle over Tontzimin between Cuncunul and Ebtún serves to illuminate the varied roles caciques and indigenous leaders of both towns played in defending the interests of their respective communities.

ECONOMIC AND SOCIOPOLITICAL BACKGROUND OF COLONIAL YUCATÁN

When Spaniards arrived in Yucatán in the sixteenth century, they were disappointed by the lack of gold and fertile land. In contrast to other core areas of Mexico, the Spaniards saw Yucatán as a frontier province, and perhaps it is because of their general disinterest in this area that Yucatán was able to survive the Conquest with its indigenous culture and society more or less intact.[4] To promote settlement of Spaniards in Yucatán, the Spanish crown offered the conquerors the incentive of becoming *encomenderos*. This system of *encomienda* was based on the notion of a tributary system whereby individual Spaniards were granted a number of indigenous people (*indígenas*) from whom they could extract tribute on the understanding that the encomenderos would also be responsible for the well-being of the indígenas under their tutelage. In Yucatán, the system of encomienda and *repartimiento* (forced sale of goods to indígenas) continued until the late eighteenth century, when the Bourbon reforms abolished both systems.

In addition to the encomienda system, the crown's policy of creating *reducciones* helped the Spanish colonial government to control and extract tribute from indígenas. Under the system of reducción, indígenas were forcibly moved from their hamlets and gathered in towns, which were under Spanish control. This system of forcible settlement served a twin purpose: it made it easier to control and thereby tax indigenous people who lived within these reducciones, and it furthered the Catholic church's desire to convert indígenas and the crown's desire to Hispanicize them. Although these policies were supposed to help the administration of indigenous communities, in reality they created disputes and struggles that would color the relationship both among different indigenous communities and between the colonial government and indigenous pueblos for at least the next three centuries.

This fact is clearly evident in the case of towns such as Ebtún and Cuncunul. In the seventeenth century, the two communities were situated in the province of Cupules, which was bordered on the west by the province of Sotuta and on the south by the province of Cochuah, in what is now the region surrounding Valladolid in northeast Yucatán. The concentration of indígenas in five pueblos—Ebtún, Cuncunul, Kaua, Tecom, and Tixcacalcupul—took place as a direct result of reducción. Yet there were continuities between pre-Conquest and colonial society as experienced by indigenous Maya. Restall believes that the reducción was not able to eliminate preexisting factionalism among Maya elite. The Maya continued to identify themselves with respect to their *cahob* (plural of cah), the fundamental units of pre-Columbian Maya society, even after reducciones took place. Thus, the new accouterments of colonial society were grafted onto the already existing cah structure in such a way that cahob continued to function as sociopolitical and territorial units. The pre-Columbian cah was a geographic entity composed of both a residential core and a territorial spread, which could lie far from the residential plots. This fact meant that "although the residential cah may have been transplanted [i.e., through reducción] the territorial cah was left intact, allowing the cabildo and landowning families of the cah to continue working and exchanging the same fields and forests."[5] For indígenas of these "reduced" towns, in some cases it meant walking for many hours to get to these lands where they could sow corn and on which they could even build makeshift houses. The dispute between Ebtún and Cuncunul arose out of such a process. In the years after the reducción, the two towns engaged in heated debate over who had the right to cultivate the lands of the territorial cah that they had been forced to leave.

Along with communal lands, there were lands that were clearly private or family property. There also appear to have been joint- or multiple-ownership situations in which several members of a family could own a particular plot of land. Unlike Spanish inheritance patterns in which land inherited by several people was divided up, in the Maya system lands were passed on to several members of the family, who held it jointly without dividing the land. This also meant that the same land was often passed down from generation to generation.[6]

In the pre-Columbian period, rival cahob and native nobility often engaged in conflict over land, and this continued even after reducciones had altered the territorial and social makeup of the countryside. The government intervened in order to settle such land disputes. This intervention was, of course, more due to colonial exigencies than to the Spanish government's desire to promote conciliation among indigenous communities. In the early colonial period, there was still plentiful land to go around given the demographic collapse of indigenous populations brought on by Old World diseases and the relatively small number of encomenderos. But the stability of indigenous land tenure was in the economic interests of the government. Indeed, the Spanish colonial government made it a point to resolve boundary disputes and validate territorial rights when implementing the encomienda and the repartimiento.[7] Although the Spanish validated territorial rights, land dynamics under colonialism often favored indigenous nobility over the mass of commoners. Under colonial rule, for instance, unlike indigenous commoners, or *macehuales*, who had usufruct rights to community land, Maya nobility had the right to own private property.[8] The coexistence of pre-Conquest territorial dynamics and Spanish practices of land tenure and ownership made for complicated disputes over land in the early colonial period.

Given the dearth of water resources in this part of Yucatán, this struggle was as much over water as over land. The most contested lands were sites of *cenotes* (sinkholes; subterranean sources of water), which are prevalent in Yucatán. The Maya valued lands with access to water over other kinds of land, even those that were better and more fertile in all other respects. The disputed Tontzimin tract, for instance, was an extension of land surrounding a cenote also called Tontzimin.

Tontzimin was additionally important because it held a cacao grove.[9] Cacao usually grows in humid and wet climates and is rare in dry areas such as Yucatán. Moreover, cacao had been a valuable cash crop from pre-Columbian times and also had functioned as currency. Indeed, evidence from the early 1700s suggests that thousands of pounds of cacao were imported into Yucatán, where there was a high demand for the commodity both for currency as well as for making chocolate.[10] Traveling in Yucatán in the early nineteenth century, John Lloyd Stephens found that cacao was still very much a part of commercial transactions among indígenas and commented that "there is no copper money in Yucatán nor any coin whatever under a medio, or a six and quarter cents and this deficiency is supplied by these grains of cacao."[11] The fact that Tontzimin was the site of a cacao grove must have made it that much more desirable by indigenous communities around it and also serves to explain why that particular piece of land became a center of contention among the different towns. When he sold the Tontzimin land in 1665, the cacique Diego Cupul described it as having a cenote with a cacao grove. This was probably no idle descriptive act; the presence of the cacao grove must have been an asset that Diego Cupul used to his advantage when selling the land.

Understanding the social and political setup of colonial Yucatán is also vital to examining the struggle over the Tontzimin tract. By the sixteenth century, the república de indios had been instituted as the sole system of indigenous government. Each república was headed by a cacique-gobernador and represented by an indigenous cabildo of officers, namely, alcaldes (judges), *regidores* (aldermen), and *escribanos* (scribes).[12] Under this system, indigenous communities enjoyed a certain degree of autonomy. The logic of having these separate repúblicas was that it eliminated the need for Spanish officials to govern the pueblos directly (a task that would have been daunting given the linguistic and cultural barriers between Spaniards and indigenous commoners). In Yucatán, the indigenous república was grafted onto the preexisting cah. Thus, each major cah acquired a cabildo, which was headed by the preexisting Maya batab. One reason for the continuation of the role of the batab was the Spanish desire to coopt pre-Conquest local leadership or nobility; with the creation of the república system, the office of batab and cacique essentially merged.

Sergio Quezada has argued that batabob functioned as the cornerstone of the early colonial system.[13] There are examples of hereditary caciques, especially in the early days of the indigenous repúblicas, but over the seventeenth century the office of gobernador, or cacique, became based on yearly elections in which indigenous cabildos decided on a suitable candidate to serve as cacique. On the whole, the Spanish government did not interfere with these elections but simply validated them. In his case study of the town of Tekantó, Thompson found that the same batab was being named each year in the elections. He found that in practice batabob appeared to have continued in office for up to twenty years (corresponding to the Maya tun calendrical system). The autonomy of the indigenous cabildos in deciding their batabob or caciques and their duration in office continued even into the late eighteenth century.

From the 1770s onward, vice-regal regulations on cabildo elections introduced the *terna* system. The cabildo of each community had to send a terna, the names of three candidates, for the position of the cacique, one of whom the government would name as the rightful cacique of the community. In practice, however, there seems to have been a tacit agreement between the government and the cabildo that whomever was named first on the list by the cabildo was the man who would be named as the cacique by the government.[14] In this way, cabildos exercised considerable power over the naming of the cacique while helping to maintain the fiction of colonial administration. Moreover, the position of cacique was something that could be achieved rather than being simply ascribed through kinship or hereditary channels. For instance, there are examples of cabildo officers such as regidores and escribanos rising up the ladder of the cabildo to become caciques.[15]

The cacique and the cabildo had several important functions. The cabildo acted as the notary, notarizing bills of sale, wills, petitions, legal proceedings, death notices, and cabildo elections. The cabildo also served as an archive containing all documents pertinent to the community. The cacique and the cabildo administered local justice, represented the community as a corporate body to outsiders, and collected tribute. The cabildo also owned and administered public utilities, maintained all public buildings, recruited and organized labor, ensured the running of the postal system (*cordillera*), administered the public granary and community treasury (*cajas de comunidad*), supported literacy, and organized festivals.[16] The cacique's main task was to foster stability in the community, and he was a central figure in the administration of the community. Caciques and officers of the indigenous repúblicas governed and collected taxes from the communities and passed it on to the Spanish officials. In return, caciques were often exempt from taxes and other contributions. These caciques also remained at the forefront of struggles over land. At the same time, it is important to acknowledge that indigenous communities were not undifferentiated units. Rather, the mass of indigenous commoners living within a community had a more or less tributary relationship with indigenous leaders and nobility.

Although indigenous communities were largely administered by their cabildos, indigenous people did have access to Spanish law as well. On the whole, the Spanish crown saw indígenas as minors and, indeed, many of the rules that applied to children in the Iberian Peninsula were superimposed on Spanish governance in Latin America. In Spain, orphans were often put under the charge of a protector who was responsible for the proper care of these children. This office of protector was reinvoked and became established in the Americas under colonial rule to ensure the welfare of *niños con barbas* (literally, children with beards), a phrase used to describe indigenous people.[17] The protector was the representative of the Tribunal de Indios, which had been established under colonial rule to provide legal aid to indígenas. The protector and other legal agents of the government drew their income from fixed salaries provided by the government. The upkeep of the legal system was ensured through taxes on all indígenas of a half-real, also known as the *holpatan*.[18] The legal system thus instituted became a cornerstone of indigenous disputes in Yucatán, and indigenous caciques became skilled at using the legal system in their own interests during the colonial period.

CACIQUES IN LATE COLONIAL EBTÚN

Historian Nancy Farriss has characterized the late colonial period as a "second conquest."[19] Although other scholars such as Mark Lentz believe that the term oversimplifies what was a much more complex reality at the local level, it is nevertheless indubitable that the Bourbon reforms of the late eighteenth century brought about important changes in Yucatán.[20] Indeed, historian D. A. Brading saw the Bourbon reforms with their attendant officials as a "revolution in government."[21]

Among the most important innovations of the Bourbon reforms was the Ordinance of Intendants (1786), which reorganized the administration of Spanish America. According to this decree, New Spain was divided into administrative units called intendancies, constituted of one or more provinces. The intendant presided over these administrative units and enjoyed broad-ranging fiscal power including overseeing the treasury and collecting taxes. Each intendancy was further divided into *subdelegaciones* with an official, the *subdelegado*, overseeing the pueblos in his subdelegación and stationed at the *cabecera* (head town) of the subdelegación. The 1786 reforms divided Yucatán into thirteen subdelegaciones: Bacalar, Beneficios Altos, Beneficios Bajos, Bolonchencauich, Camino Real Alto, Camino Real Bajo, Campeche, Costa, Mérida, Sahcabchén, Sierra, Tizimín, and Valladolid.[22] The Bourbon reforms, which were meant to centralize and streamline administration of the colonies, rooted out practices of encomienda and repartimiento; in the person of the subdelegado, the arms of the government reached further into the internal workings of indigenous pueblos than had ever been the case.[23] After the 1780s, for instance, people of Ebtún and Cuncunul could travel less than ten kilometers to meet the subdelegado in Valladolid, thus making it possible for more frequent and simpler access to the colonial government. Compared to land agreements and disputes of the preceding two centuries among the five pueblos recorded in the Ebtún documents, we now find the involvement of a much larger number of Spanish officials. What previously would have been a case resolved simply by caciques and other indigenous leaders now was referred to Spanish authorities with mixed results.

As the *Titles of Ebtun* documents show, encroachments on neighboring land were frequent in the late colonial period.[24] Caciques and other indigenous leaders were valued members of the community and were indispensable in disputes over land and scarce resources. At a basic level, caciques functioned as validators. The knowledge that caciques possessed of their lands was almost unparalleled in their communities, as illustrated by the vignette at the beginning of this chapter, in which the caciques were in an instant able to draw a map of their lands from memory alone. In terms of land struggle, this meant that these indigenous leaders became valuable in settling boundary disputes by drawing on their superior knowledge of both the terrain of their lands and their inhabitants but also from their knowledge of the community's past. Thus, caciques and justicias were customarily summoned to the door of the *audiencia* (audience chamber) in the municipal building to reconcile boundary maps of one community with those of others.[25]

Even after caciques gave up their positions by retiring or relinquishing their charge, they continued to be important in their communities precisely because they could remember the events and facts concerning land use and ownership from their time. Thus ex-caciques too could be summoned to validate territorial divisions and maps, and in this way their knowledge ensured their continued importance in their communities. For example, after boundary disputes erupted between Yaxcabá and the towns of Ebtún, Kaua, Tekom, Cuncunul, and Tixcacalcupul in 1764, the ex-cacique of Sotuta, Don Gerónimo Cocom, was summoned in 1775 to validate the boundary map separating the lands of the respective communities.[26]

Though we have no documents that directly relate to the struggle over the Tontzimin tract before 1797, later documents suggest that although Cuncunul had officially come to possess the Tontzimin tract in 1725 this did not deter the people of Ebtún from encroaching on that site. In 1797 the protector, Agustín Crespo, charged the cacique and authorities of Ebtún with intruding into the lands of Cuncunul, interfering with the old landmarks, and placing new ones and cultivating that land. Crespo appealed to the governor in a petition to ensure that the people of Ebtún were restrained from encroaching on Cuncunul's possessions. In response, Governor O'Neill appointed Manuel de Arze, a Spanish judge of Uayma, to investigate the matter and correct the trespass.[27]

On receiving the governor's order, Manuel de Arze set off from Uayma and on 5 September summoned the caciques of Ebtún and Cuncunul to accompany him in a survey of the land to settle the dispute. This act of conducting a survey in the presence of a cacique was a well-established norm and can be seen in many parts of Yucatán during this time. Caciques often walked the whole length of a plot of land placing landmarks and demarcating that territory from those of its neighbors. What made this particular survey special was that here the caciques did not occupy a neutral role of demarcating land (if indeed, such neutrality is ever possible) but rather represented two communities that opposed each other and for both of whom the result of the survey could have important consequences. What would have been a fairly routine operation became a tense and charged event.

At the beginning of his survey, Manuel de Arze asked the authorities of Ebtún who had gathered there to show him the map or documents pertaining to the forests of their community. Since the leaders of Ebtún had neither, De Arze proceeded on the survey using the maps that the authorities of Cuncunul had brought with them. What followed provides us with an important glimpse into the role of caciques. At four in the afternoon the party of the leaders of both towns, De Arze, and probably, though he is not mentioned, an interpreter for De Arze arrived at the cenote at Cosil, "where an old landmark was found which is cited by the instruments [i.e., maps or documents] of the said people of Cuncunul." Manuel de Arze again urged the people of Ebtún to show him their documents, and they replied that they did not have them. Later, in his report De Arze wrote: "And from the well of Cosil, which belongs to the people of Ebtún, they [the authorities of Ebtún] took leave of me and went back along the line I had identified, to demolish an old landmark. The following day I repaired it."[28]

Whether as validators of knowledge or in any other role, caciques were important in land struggles because of their status as representatives of their communities and their standing as mediators for their pueblos. Yet this mediation was not of a passive kind, in which caciques simply acted as conduits or messengers. Rather, as this example of Manuel de Arze's survey shows, the caciques were active agents in their role as intermediaries. The leaders of Ebtún represented their community and went along with the survey, but they were also strategic and cunning. These leaders who themselves had no maps to help them used the survey to identify old landmarks and then undermined Cuncunul's chance of success by demolishing one of them. The cacique and other leaders of Ebtún did not simply act as intermediaries between the community of Ebtún and the Spanish government (represented by Manuel de Arze); they actively attempted to influence the outcome of this meeting in favor of their pueblo even if it meant doing something blatantly illegal during a government-sponsored survey.

On 8 September, Manuel de Arze concluded his survey and decided in favor of Cuncunul. In his report he emphasized that the people of Ebtún did not have documents to prove their ownership of the lands on which they were encroaching, and for this reason he had "notified them that they should not again cultivate the said lands contrary to the wish of the people of Cuncunul."[29] Though we know from De Arze's report about the actions of the leaders of Ebtún, one wonders what role the cacique and justicias of Cuncunul played in this outcome. We know that the leaders of Cuncunul accompanied De Arze for the entire duration of the survey, whereas the leaders of Ebtún left by four in the afternoon on the first day of the survey. Did this give leverage to the leaders of Cuncunul, who—in the absence of any leader from Ebtún—could steer the survey toward a favorable outcome? We do know, for instance, that after De Arze discovered that the Ebtún group had demolished a landmark the leaders of Cuncunul expressed to him that "those of Ebtún have been accustomed to demolish landmarks in the forests."[30] We can also wonder how De Arze could have found out about the landmark, which he had already passed, unless the men from Cuncunul informed him that the caciques of Ebtún had demolished it. We know that there was no eyewitness to the demolition of the landmark. Yet De Arze had no doubt that the leaders of Ebtún were responsible, suggesting that the leaders of Cuncunul had influenced him. Again, then, accompanying Manuel de Arze on his survey was not a passive act for these caciques; rather, the survey was a window of opportunity in which they could influence the government's decision, however subtly, in their favor.

In response to Manuel de Arze's report and Agustín Crespo's subsequent petition asking for Ebtún to be restrained from trespassing on Cuncunul's lands, the governor of Yucatán ordered in favor of Cuncunul.[31] In October 1797 the governor's decision was communicated to the people of Ebtún, who agreed to abide by it, bringing an end—at least on paper—to this episode of land struggle between the two towns.

This was a short-lived peace. In 1800 (the exact date is not recorded) the town of Ebtún began a lawsuit against Cuncunul, once again over the Tontzimin tract. The cacique and justicias of Ebtún appealed to the governor to let their community buy Tontzimin from Cuncunul and argued that certain individuals of their town had originally sold the tract to Cuncunul for the sum of twenty-five pesos—but had done so without the knowledge of the cacique of Ebtún.[32] Using the documents available, it appears that this refers to the sale of Tontzimin by Diego Chay of Ebtún to Diego Cupul of Cuncunul in 1638.[33] Now, in 1800, the leaders of Ebtún invoked this sale, which had taken place more than a hundred and fifty years before, to persuade the government to let it buy back the Tontzimin tract for the same amount. The leaders of Ebtún argued that, since the site of Tontzimin was within the radius of their own community and more than nine leagues from that of Cuncunul, Ebtún needed the land more than did Cuncunul.

Upon the requests of the governor and the protector, the case was passed on to the subdelegado in Valladolid, Ignacio Rivas.[34] In December 1801, Rivas summoned the indigenous leaders of Ebtún and Cuncunul to appear before him in Valladolid. The result of this hearing proved to be a surprise. Whereas in 1797 the government had decided in favor of Cuncunul in the struggle over the Tontzimin tract, Rivas now reported to the governor that he had "ascertained that under the pretext of a parcel of land named Tontzimin which the former (i.e., Cuncunul) purchased for twenty-five pesos, (Cuncunul) has usurped two other parcels of land, Cosil and Kochila which are contiguous to it, from Ebtún."[35] Now, rather than being the instigator of conflict, Ebtún was suddenly in the role of the wronged.

We know that during the survey conducted by Manuel de Arze, the leaders of Ebtún had declared in the presence of the people of Cuncunul that they had no relevant maps or documents. Ignacio de Rivas, in his report, hinted that with the knowledge that Ebtún had no documents to prove their case the people of Cuncunul had unrestrainedly established new landmarks in the land that was actually a part of Ebtún. Of course, the fact that Ebtún had no documents begs the question of how Rivas was able to arrive at that conclusion. Unfortunately, we have no documents to show us how Rivas was convinced, but it perhaps would not be wrong to say that the cacique and justicias of Ebtún must have presented their case to Rivas exceedingly well, thus demonstrating their prowess as negotiators and mediators for their community.

The cacique and other leaders of Cuncunul did not accept this new development passively but rather immediately petitioned the protector to restrain the people of Ebtún from trespassing on the Tontzimin tract. They argued that their former caciques had sold it to the Spaniards but that the community had later reacquired it since they needed the tract for their farming. They also emphasized that the government itself had validated their possession of the Tontzimin tract: "Four years ago Don Manuel Arze, by commission of the Superior Government, delivered it [Tontzimin] to us with the instruments." The leaders of Cuncunul also informed the protector that "we have [notified] the people of Ebtún that they should not farm in the said forests and [that] they should pay their rentals."[36]

To resolve this situation, the protector summoned leaders of both towns to Mérida in February 1802. The vignette that begins this chapter captures this episode where both sides met outside the governor's court with the protector and tried to come to an amicable solution. The outcome of this episode was that on 15 February 1802, the governor ordered Cuncunul to sell the Tontzimin tract to Ebtún for twenty-five pesos.[37] The subdelegado was instructed to draw from the community funds of Ebtún and deposit the money into the communal funds of Cuncunul. Both pueblos were told to confine themselves within the old boundaries of their territories. For the government, this result represented an equitable decision. Further, members of the government such as the minister of the exchequer felt that "recognition of these [former boundaries], or of their mutual boundaries, apart from the questions which arise from the portion sold, should leave them without grounds for litigation inspired by ill-will as well as the continual travelling back and forth, from which they perhaps receive a detriment greater than the benefit which is the object of their conspiracy."[38]

A stable countryside with clear demarcations of communities and property was in the interest of the government since it allowed for the smooth operation of colonial economic mechanisms such as tax collection. It did not hurt that, after years of dealing with the conflict and litigation between Ebtún and Cuncunul, the government wanted to put the matter to rest swiftly by prescribing that each community stay within its original boundaries. Thus, the members of the community of Ebtún were asked to "make free use of the site of Tontzimin," and those of Cuncunul were warned not to disturb or harm them.[39] So there would be no future litigations concerning the Tontzimin tract, the subdelegado, Ignacio de Rivas, commissioned another Spanish official, Andrés Mariano Peniche (later secretary to Governor Miguel de Castro y Araos), to survey the boundaries between Ebtún and Cuncunul.

On 16 March 1802, Peniche—accompanied by two witnesses and an interpreter—began his survey of the lands "usurped [by Cuncunul] from the community of Ebtún under the pretext of Tontzimin."[40] The leaders of the town of Kaua joined him. From other documents we know that Ebtún and Kaua had always had a close relationship, and it is likely that the leaders of Kaua were not neutral bystanders during the survey but would have sided with Ebtún. On the other hand, we learn that despite numerous summons by Peniche the cacique and indigenous authorities of Cuncunul refused to accompany him on the survey. They did appear at the beginning of the survey but then left. It is important to ask why Cuncunul refused to stay. Although the documents themselves do not provide us with any definite answer to explain the Cuncunul leaders' behavior, it is possible to draw some inferences. The leaders of Cuncunul probably felt that they would not be able to change the outcome of the survey, since Commissioner Peniche and the government more generally seemed convinced that Cuncunul had usurped lands from Ebtún. In fact, the leaders of Cuncunul were already devising a counterplan to get back their lands. This intention becomes clear when the protector appealed on 28 April 1802 to the governor to give the people of Cuncunul a hearing.[41] Sure that Commissioner Peniche was already convinced that they had usurped the lands of Ebtún, the leaders of Cuncunul wasted no time participating in the survey but rather concentrated their energy on communicating with the protector and convincing him to present their case before the government.

Commissioner Peniche decided his survey in favor of Ebtún: "I ordered [landmarks of Cuncunul] to be demolished, indicating the lands have been examined and belong only to the government of the said town of Ebtún."[42] On 28 April, possibly at the instigation of the leaders of Cuncunul, the protector Crespo challenged this decision, arguing that before the survey the leaders of Cuncunul had come before the commissioner and left their documents and maps with the latter. The protector wrote to the governor that in the documents, which the leaders of Cuncunul had left behind at the start of the survey (presumably to Peniche), "it is evident that they [Cuncunul] have a just claim to various sites of land." Crespo also accused Peniche of favoritism, saying that "it is evident from them [i.e., foregoing proceedings] that a survey has been made [i.e., survey by Peniche] without its being ordered, but at the request of the people of Ebtún."[43] Crespo argued that the people of Cuncunul should be given a hearing before the matter was settled.

This particular episode is our key to understanding the role of caciques and other indigenous leaders in community disputes in the late colonial period. Most poignant is the fact that such leaders allied with certain representatives of the government to achieve their objectives. For instance, the people of Ebtún understood that they needed to ally with Peniche, and Crespo championed the cause of Cuncunul. In other words, these disputes and how they became resolved often depended on personal relationships with government officials. The fact that caciques made these connections and used them to their advantage shows that they were not simply intermediaries in a neutral sense, that instead their intermediation was essentially of a political nature. And in the process of mediation they often influenced its very outcome. It is probably not a coincidence that the decision always came in favor of the town whose leaders were present for the most time during the survey and accompanied the surveyor.

On 31 December 1802, the protector Crespo tried to bring an end to the conflict over the Tontzimin tract by suggesting that the land be divided between the two towns. It is not hard to see that Crespo's decision was influenced by the leaders of Cuncunul, who were "unanimous and agreed in proposing that they would favor the people of Ebtún by granting them half of the said site."[44] For the cacique and authorities of Cuncunul this compromise probably represented the only option they had for retaining some part of the Tontzimin tract in the face of the commissioner's and the attorney general of the natives' (*procurador general de los naturales*) clear stance in favor of Ebtún. Cuncunul's offer, however generous it seemed to be in the eyes of Crespo, did not find a similar enthusiasm with the attorney general, Juan Esteban de Meneses, who asserted that "it is plain that in the attempt to cede half the land to Ebtún gratis and without payment, so that they [Cuncunul] might continue to usurp the lands, as they have done, under cover of the other half which they would have left, [what they really have in view is the evasion of the] determinate [decree] already cited."[45]

Once again, facing a legal deadlock where the attorney general and the protector were arguing for opposite lines of action, the governor referred the matter to the lieutenant assessor, Miguel Sandoval.[46] In 1804–5 (the exact date is unknown), Don Miguel Sandoval confirmed the decree of February 1802 that the sum of twenty-five pesos be drawn from the community funds of Ebtún to pay Cuncunul for the Tontzimin tract. However, he disagreed with the result of Peniche's survey since it had been performed at the sole request of the cacique and other leaders of Ebtún, and "it is considered to be importunately executed by the Subdelegate of the Department and without the judicial decree of this government." Sandoval declared Peniche's survey to be "void and of no effect."[47] This decision looks to have concluded this part of the struggle over the Tontzimin tract.

Nevertheless, the struggle over Tontzimin continued, and a few years later (exact date is unknown) the cacique and justicias of Cuncunul again appealed to government officials for a survey of the Tontzimin tract.[48] The leaders of Cuncunul obviously believed that despite Sandoval's decision some people from Ebtún were continuing to encroach on their lands. The cacique of Ebtún, Don Pedro Pat, met with the cacique of Cuncunul, Don Juan Chan, along with other members of the indigenous cabildos of both pueblos at Mérida in July 1812.[49] For what seems to be one of the longest periods of negotiation we know of between the two towns, the leaders spent eight days together negotiating over the Tontzimin tract. The documents are silent on what the leaders of the two towns said to each other. Nor do we know whether there was any third party such as a government official present at this meeting. The only information we have is from a short note by Don Pedro Pat saying that Don Juan Chan had agreed to drop his suit against Ebtún.

Sometimes silences can speak volumes. Here, we find for the first time a real effort by both towns to come to an agreement. Both caciques obviously played key roles in this negotiation. The actual note written by Chan was in Mayan, and we don't find any document from any Spanish official mentioning this meeting at all. Given the Spanish government's proclivity to record and preserve all developments, the fact that there is no document in Spanish describing this meeting seems to suggest—although we will never know for certain—that the two towns negotiated with each other directly without the presence of any Spaniard. This eight-day negotiation highlights something very important: that the caciques and other indigenous leaders continued to exercise a fundamentally political role as intermediaries between pueblos and that, even in 1812 on the eve of the first abolition of the indigenous repúblicas in Yucatán, caciques could function as self-sufficient political agents representing their communities.

The extant documents concerning the struggle over the Tontzimin tract extend to the year 1820. The final years saw the familiar back-and-forth, with Cuncunul asking for another survey and the government striving to resolve this conflict through means of reports and investigations by intermediaries (surveyors and commissioners) and government officials. While much of this was reminiscent of the past, we can also see signs of increasing desperation among the communities to hold onto their lands. We see examples of extralegal means used by communities such as fraud and impersonation to achieve their ends. On 15 August 1819, Don Pedro Pat and other leaders of Ebtún informed the protector, Don Juan de Dios Cosgaya, that documents pertaining to the land owned by Ebtún had been stolen by men of Cuncunul from the office of the secretary of the government in Mérida. Pedro Pat described the deception perpetrated by Cuncunul: "Bernardo Chan and Ángel Tamay of Cuncunul appeared and said how they were Ebtún men, to deceive Don Antonio Barceles. That was what they made out; they were not of Ebtún, they were of Cuncunul."[50] The fact that these men had been commissioned by the cacique and other indigenous leaders of the town of Cuncunul to perpetrate this deception can be concluded from the fact that the indigenous república of Cuncuncul was subsequently found to be in possession of these documents; the subdelegado, Juan José Galvez, recovered these documents from them on 2 September 1819.[51] Rather than follow legal means to redress their grievances, leaders of Cuncunul had stooped to deception and subterfuge. This episode throws open the question of whether there ever really could be a lasting peace between these two towns. After all, the same caciques—Don Pedro Pat and Don Juan Chan—had been involved in 1812 in an eight-day negotiation that had concluded on amicable terms. Yet eight years on, they were back in the game of one-upmanship, with Chan commissioning impersonators essentially to steal Ebtún's documents. Although *The Titles of Ebtun* does not provide any documentary evidence of it after 1820, the preceding episodes of conflict suggest strongly that this struggle over the Tontzimin tract must have continued and perhaps intensified in the post-independence period.

CACIQUES AND EVERYDAY RESISTANCE

After the Bourbon reforms, the hand of the colonial government reached farther into the lives of indigenous people through interventions into village disputes by government officials such as subdelegados. In some cases these officials intervened at the request of indígenas themselves, but in others their presence was seen as unwelcome interference in issues that had always been resolved internally by indigenous leaders of communities. No doubt certain indigenous leaders must have felt that these officials were stepping on their toes. Yet open conflict or resistance to these interventions would have been undesirable, since the caciques retained their position by cooperating with the colonial government. Anthropologist James Scott posits that to understand resistance we need to look at the daily interactions and everyday ways in which subaltern populations challenge authority.[52] Other theorists such as Ranajit Guha have argued that we need to read documents against the grain in order to understand the silences and to recover the acts of resistance that are not recognized as such by authorities.[53] We can use these insights to understand the behavior of caciques.

In *The Titles of Ebtun* we find instances of caciques demolishing landmarks, leaving midway during a survey, or not showing up to a survey even when they have been expressly summoned by the authorities. We need to see these actions not as illogical, vindictive, or apathetic but rather as acts of resistance to colonial authorities. Raymond Craib sees similar actions of villagers in nineteenth-century Mexico with regard to the act of surveying land by the government and writes: "Villagers had a clear enough idea of how the survey worked to know that its potential effects could be undermined without resorting to outright confrontation, which would expose them to retaliation. Thus, in lieu of running the surveyor out of town, they often destroyed station points, pulled up posts, and altered the locations of landmarks."[54] Acts of resistance can also be gleaned from reports of Spanish officials in which we find that caciques declared themselves to be satisfied with the result of the surveys, only later to engage surreptitiously in acts of subterfuge and conflict.

The hubris of Spanish officials—that through their superior powers of reasoning and persuasion they could bring order to the indigenous world and even solve the internal disputes of indigenous people—can be seen in various documents. In June 1700, a Spanish official, Antonio de Argaiz, arrived in Zaka, a league from Tekom, where he was met by the caciques and justicias of the five towns of Tekom, Cuncunul, Tixcacal, Kaua, and Ebtún. Together this band of men walked the lands with Argaiz setting up landmarks to identify the boundaries of their lands and the limits of their possessions. In his report, Argaiz presented the survey as a success, and his pride in the fact that he had been able to bring all these towns to harmonious agreement is apparent. He was obviously pleased that "they all replied unanimously that they were satisfied and that they had nothing to ask for, because to each had been given what was his, according to the places mentioned in their titles." He smugly noted that "in my presence they embraced, promising in the future not to engage in litigation or in any other affair in regard to this matter. All this I did by virtue of his Majesty's Tribunal."[55]

We see this again during Antonio de Arze's survey of 1764, when all the caciques "unanimously agreed" with the surveyor's decisions regarding boundary divisions.[56] This sort of compliance can also be seen in reports by subdelegados, who recorded the reactions of caciques after decisions by the government were announced.[57] Yet the notion that these Spanish officials had solved these problems proved illusory when time and again the indigenous people engaged in conflict and subterfuge over the disputed lands. It is likely that when caciques said they were "satisfied" they were simply paying lip service to the government officials and trying to bring the government intervention to an end as quickly as possible. The multiple and repeated acts of encroachment and conflict that these towns engaged in throw serious doubt on the supposed success of government interventions. Instead, the verbal and overt compliance with government actions hid the actual intentions of these caciques, which became expressed in their actions on the ground, whether acts of encroachment or theft.

PERSONAL AS POLITICAL

The most important aspect of the relationship between indigenous communities and the colonial government was undoubtedly the fact that it was experienced in a very personal way. The documents of *The Titles of Ebtun* show with remarkable clarity that caciques and other indigenous leaders experienced the government through their lived and everyday interactions with the government's representatives on the ground. The personal relationships and alliances forged between the indigenous leaders and particular colonial officials meant that at certain times different layers of bureaucracy would rub against each other, sparking conflict.

An example can be seen during the clash between Ebtún and Cuncunul in 1802 described above over the proposal to divide the Tontzimin tract. On 16 March 1802, Commissioner Don Andrés Mariano Peniche undertook a survey of the lands of Ebtún. Despite various summons the cacique and other leaders of Cuncunul did not accompany Peniche as he surveyed the land. At the end of the survey, Peniche gave Ebtún possession of the disputed land. The subdelegado at that time, Ignacio de Rivas, delivered the papers of the survey to the leaders of Ebtún and asked them to take them to the governor-intendant in Mérida so that the he could make a final decision and settle the dispute.[58] A few days later the protector of natives, Agustín Crespo, petitioned the governor protesting the legality of Peniche's survey. In this petition, Crespo accused Peniche of favoritism, asserting that the survey had been undertaken solely on the request of the leaders of Ebtún and not any government authority. For his own part, Crespo presented the case of Cuncunul and proposed to divide the Tontzimin tract between the two towns. In this Crespo was undoubtedly revealing his alliance with Cuncunul, since such a division would clearly favor Cuncunul, who by Peniche's survey stood to lose all the disputed lands. This clear dissonance among the layers of colonial bureaucracy is further highlighted in the attorney general for Indians' response to Crespo's suggestion. Juan Esteban de Meneses asserted that the survey had been commissioned by the subdelegado and, "by his [Crespo's] representations . . . he [Crespo] stirred up this town and that of Ebtún which had been pacified by the decision [i.e., earlier decision of Cuncunul to sell Tontzimin to Ebtún]."[59]

This episode shows two important things. We see that caciques allied with particular officials to achieve their ends; Cuncunul allied with its protector, and Ebtún allied with the commissioner. Therefore, favoritism and alliance formation linked caciques to specific officials in a very personal way. Additionally, we see that different branches of government or layers of bureaucracy could come into conflict with each other, further negating any sort of simple mediation or decision making at the government level.[60] This example also portrays the relationships between government and caciques as nonlinear and nonuniversal; they were, instead, relationships defined by personal considerations particular to each official and each indigenous cabildo. Here, the personal was indeed the political.

Actions of caciques become intelligible when we understand that in late colonial society the government did not loom in the background in the way that we think of a nation-state; instead, its presence was felt and negotiated in everyday interactions with government functionaries. In 1764, when Antonio de Arze set out on his survey of the boundary between the lands of Yaxcabá and those of Ebtún, Kaua, Tekom, Cuncunul, and Tixcacal, he encountered the cacique and justicias of the town of Tiholop, who joined Arze uninvited.[61] These caciques had not appeared out of simply curiosity but rather because they were afraid that if they were not present their interests could be compromised. The wisdom of the Tiholop caciques becomes apparent as we study the dispute between Ebtún and Cuncunul from 1797 to 1820. In each case without exception it was the community whose cacique spent the most time in the company of the surveyor who received the favorable decision in the outcome of the survey. What the caciques of Tiholop knew intuitively and from experience was that being present was half the battle.

At the same time, some caciques did take advantage of the new mechanisms of government and, for a few, intervention into their communal disputes by government officials proved beneficial. Within the regional context of the towns of Ebtún and Cuncunul, indigenous people saw government to be constituted in the person of the governor, who resided in Mérida, and down the bureaucratic ladder in the person of the subdelegado who lived closer in the city of Valladolid. Most of the time, the indígenas of Cuncunul, Ebtún, and the surrounding towns experienced the colonial government in their own localities through other government intermediaries such as surveyors, interpreters, and transcribers and through legal intermediaries of the Tribunal de Indios such as protectors. Once again, the personal nature of these interactions must be stressed. Certain surveyors were seen as allies by particular caciques, or at least as more sympathetic to their cause and hence more likely to favor their particular community over another's. The complexity of mapping on the ground was created by the fact that the surveyor had to rely on local knowledge for a great part of his work. Caciques undoubtedly took advantage of this along with their personal alliances with the surveyors to "fix" the boundaries of their town in a way that actually augmented the land holdings of their communities. Just to give one example, without the intervention of Spanish officials, it is unlikely that the caciques of Ebtún could have acquired the Tontzimin tract from Cuncunul for twenty-five pesos in 1802.

Also, though we obviously (obvious because the documents are mostly written by Spanish officials) don't see any of it in the documents, we need to address the question of corruption. Rather than viewing Spanish officials as disinterested mediums of the government, we need to visualize them as individuals who faced their own particular hardships. The wealth of Spanish officials in colonial Yucatán had been derived from their profits from encomienda and repartimiento. Under the Bourbons in late eighteenth century, both mechanisms of profit making were abolished, leaving Spanish officials more vulnerable and increasingly desperate to make ends meet. The Bourbon reforms attempted to address the question of corruption at the level of the governor (or intendant, as he was now also called) by raising his salary from 4,000 to 7,000 pesos annually.[62] This increase in salary was meant to give governors a high standard of living and therefore to make it unnecessary for them to engage in corruption or bribery. But no such safety net was established for subdelegados or other Spanish officials, and in the absence of repartimiento or encomienda it is not surprising that corruption could become a way out for some of these individuals.[63] We can read in secondary sources that the cabildos of Valladolid and Campeche alleged in 1795 that subdelegados under the regime of Governor O'Neill were continuing to extract repartimiento illegally.[64] If true, this conclusively indicates the existence of corruption at the local levels of Spanish colonial government in the late eighteenth century. Whether or not we have direct evidence of this in the Ebtún documents, the economic reality puts in perspective certain Spanish officials' behaviors such as favoritism and patron-client relationships with caciques and indigenous communities.

What was the world of the cacique like in the era before men like Andrés Canché inherited the office in the early national period? Examining the struggle over the Tontzimin tract emphasizes that caciques in the late colonial period were not neutral intermediaries. Rather, the role of the cacique was highly political, whereby caciques interacted with government officials, Spanish entrepreneurs, and caciques of other pueblos in ways that actually shaped the outcome of these mediations.[65] Even the simple act of walking with a surveyor along the length of a piece of land was a profoundly political act for the cacique who used this opportunity to converse with the surveyor and influence the outcome of the survey in his community's favor. Caciques and their communities' understanding of the government were shaped by their everyday interactions with Spanish officials. Thus, for colonial caciques personal relations became key to political outcomes. The cacique and the república remained central to community matters, with caciques functioning as validators of knowledge and practices and remaining at the forefront of struggles over land and resources.

CHAPTER 2

Webs of Power

Cacique Politicization in Post-Independence Yucatán

Located 170 kilometers east of Mérida, Cenotillo, as its name suggests, is a municipality of many sinkholes. The cabecera has one main cenote, but the region as a whole boasts more than a hundred of these geological formations, making it an occasional tourist spot. Back in the early nineteenth century, though, these cenotes were probably responsible for a spate of deaths from cholera, a water-borne disease that originated in India but then traveled rapidly into the Americas in the 1830s.[1] It was thus that global webs of trade and travel that connected Asia with Europe and the Americas conspired to bring Andrés Canché to the post of cacique of Cenotillo in 1834.

In 1833 the subdelegado of Valladolid drew up a list of names of possible replacements for the cacique of Cenotillo who had succumbed to cholera.[2] The governor recommended the first of those named on the list to the post of cacique, following a custom established in the colonial times that allowed communities to highlight their own chosen candidate. More than the cholera epidemic, though, what Andrés Canché would have to contend with was a new order of things.

By the time of independence, the parish of Cenotillo registered some 1,500 *vecinos* (nonindigenous residents) and around 2,500 *indios* (natives).[3] It was thus quite a Hispanicized town even though set in the east, far from the more established Spanish towns of the northwest. It is to be expected that the effects of the municipal revolution would thus be felt keenly in this area. Indeed, by the 1830s the effect of municipalization was palpable in Yucatecan pueblos. Areas previously left to the sole administration of caciques now saw the progressive incursion of government officials such as alcaldes and jueces de paz. Caciques who had previously been authorities in their towns now became more and more dependent on the goodwill of these new state officials to survive.

For Canché, the effects of municipalization would be particularly dire. On 20 February 1836, the alcalde concilidador of Cenotillo, Juan José Barrera, initiated a case against him, alleging that he and his scribe Feliciano Couoh had embezzled public money.[4] Barrera began his investigations allegedly after he found discrepancies in the amount of money corresponding to the personal tax collected by the cacique from residents of Cenotillo and the actual number of residents who claimed to have paid their taxes. When the tax defaulters, among them vecinos Baltazar Canché and Esteban Polanco, were questioned, they testified that they had already paid their own and their servants' taxes to the cacique. The truth of their statements seemed to be corroborated by the receipts they had kept after handing over their tax payments to the cacique.

For Canché and Couoh the case had immediate repercussions. Having already suffered prison time after the embezzlement had been allegedly corroborated, the two were further punished by removal from their posts, and in September 1836 authorities in Valladolid declared them unfit to hold office for another three years.[5] This would be the first of many trials that Canché would have to face in what would be the one of the longest tenures of a cacique in the history of nineteenth-century Yucatán.

A CHANGING DYNAMIC

When he rose to the post of cacique in 1834, Canché arrived into a changed world. Just a decade previously things had been very different. Even in the 1820s caciques had managed to retain much of their older privileges: case in point, the cacique of Izamal, Francisco Chí.

In 1825, Chí was asked to provide justice for old Sebastián Chan. The latter's son had had come home in the night and slapped and beaten his old father at the instigation of his wife. It was an insult that could not be easily forgotten or forgiven. Sebastián knew that the only person in the community who could give him the justice that he sought was the cacique of the town, Francisco Chí.

On paper, Chí's powers were limited. The Constitution of Cádiz in force in 1812–14 and again in 1820–21 had established ayuntamientos in towns with more than a thousand residents but also left open the option of establishing such bodies in smaller pueblos.[6] In Yucatán this meant that, technically, after 1812 the old indigenous repúblicas in pueblos were replaced by the newly established ayuntamientos. Caciques ceased to exist in legal terms, although they continued to function in practice in certain communities. The ayuntamientos held the possibility of political participation of both indigenous and non-indigenous residents. In practice, however, nonindigenous people controlled most of the newly established ayuntamientos.[7]

Tax collection proved to be the Achilles heel of the new ayuntamientos. Traditionally caciques and their repúblicas had provided an efficient means of tax collection. The caciques were sufficiently close to the indigenous residents of the pueblos that it was relatively easy for them to collect taxes. Moreover, as Yucatecan legislators lamented, these caciques seem to have collected taxes with far less corruption than was now the case with the ayuntamiento officers.[8] To solve this quandary, by 1824 the Yucatecan government had reinstated the old indigenous repúblicas but with significantly limited power. The caciques were retained in their position but were now little more than glorified tax collectors in the eyes of the government.

Despite this official proscription of power, however, villagers continued to see their cacique as the community leader. Caciques too saw themselves as fulfilling a role that was not limited to being simply a government functionary or glorified tax collector. Rather like batabob of yore, the caciques in 1825 saw themselves as defenders of the values of their community. It was thus that Sebastián approached Francisco Chí, who intervened in the domestic quarrels of the Chan family and ordered Rafael to be punished with twelve lashes and his wife with five for insulting and assaulting old Sebastián Chan.[9] When Chí's actions were challenged by Rafael, the *fiscal* (prosecutor) in charge of this case supported Chí by asserting that according to the established laws, and even the age-old "Siete Partidas," if a child abused his parent then he could be punished and that punishment would be decided by the juez or chief.[10]

The Sebastián Chan case illustrates the importance of the cacique as a primary administrator of justice as late as 1825, but things were changing rapidly. Yucatán's state constitution of 1825 firmly established the institution of ayuntamientos, creating a kind of dual government in the localities. The ayuntamientos were put in charge of the majority of administrative matters in the pueblos. The insertion of these agencies and their attendant officials such as alcaldes brought rapid change in the internal governance of pueblos and changed the face of village politics. Although indigenous residents of towns had the freedom to vote for ayuntamiento officials, a literacy requirement meant that the actual officials found eligible to serve in these bodies were mostly nonindigenous.[11]

Alcaldes came into daily contact with residents of the pueblos. They were in charge of policing and protecting the residents, promoting schools, preserving common supplies of grain, building and maintaining streets and public works, and promoting agriculture and commerce. In addition, they performed judicial functions including trying cases of petty crimes or property. In the centralist years (1829–31 and 1835–41), another government official, the juez de paz, became prominent in the countryside, but the alcaldes seem to have continued to exist, sometimes becoming jueces de paz themselves. However, unlike the elected alcaldes, the jueces were appointed officials. Moreover, unlike alcaldes, who had clearly demarcated roles, the jueces often involved themselves in the realm of duties legally under the indigenous repúblicas, such as tax collection.[12]

In addition to these officials the subdelegado, who represented the regional level, also came into frequent contact with the indígenas and especially the república members such as caciques. These officials were in a supervisory role to the indigenous repúblicas and were responsible, for instance, for overseeing república elections.[13] Certain individuals were called on to fulfill dual roles of subdelegado and juez de paz. Finally, there was the jefe político—referred to at certain periods as the *prefecto*—who had broad powers of governance and interceded when other officials failed to meet goals.[14] These jefes became particularly prominent in the centralist years, and the jefe político was one of the offices that remained important even in the late nineteenth century under the Porfiriato.[15]

By the 1830s these government officials were entrenched within the local society. As representatives of indigenous communities, caciques came into increasingly frequent contact with these officials. At a practical level, local government officials and indigenous repúblicas often shared the audiencia building and interacted on a daily basis. It was thus that José María Moo, an officer of the indigenous república of Bokobá, became a key witness to abuses conducted in the audiencia by alcalde Cecilio Sosa.[16] In real terms, especially in towns with both indigenous and nonindigenous populations, the caciques became enmeshed with greater intensity than before in politics that now involved not only their communities but also state-appointed officials.

A case from Sotuta is an interesting example of the new local dynamics. In 1837 the cacique of Sotuta found Alejandra Ek begging on the streets in the nude. A widow, Ek needed to support herself and her son. Instead of involving himself directly in the case, the cacique sought the help of the subdelegado, Policarpo Echanové, to extricate Ek's son from her with a view to removing him from a life of "scandalous idleness." Echanové obliged, sending the son to the house of one Antonio Lavalle, an "honorable" establishment where Echanové claimed he would be educated and get the chance of becoming a useful citizen.[17] Here, as in the 1825 Izamal case, the cacique intervened in the personal lives of the indigenous residents. But unlike the 1825 case, in which the cacique took it on himself to flog the offenders, in this case the cacique took no action other than using the subdelegado as the means to extricate the child from his mother. Whether the cacique's intention was indeed to provide a better home for the child or to supply Lavalle with a servant is uncertain. What is certain is that by the 1830s caciques had come to rely on government officials for ordering daily life in the community. Whereas in 1825 the cacique could take justice into his own hands, so to speak, by 1837 he relied on officials such as the subdelegado to take the actions necessary.

Traveling through the village of Nohcacab, John Lloyd Stephens and Frederick Catherwood witnessed the ceremony associated with municipal elections in early national Yucatán. A crowd of Maya in clean dresses had gathered in the plaza while "Indian" women and

Hispanic "ladies" stood in front of the church to welcome the procession of newly elected officials. The padre led the procession, and behind him walked the white alcaldes in their black body coats and black hats, looking somber and aloof from the crowd in their white dresses and straw hats. Then followed the Maya officials, each holding his staff of office and, finally, the rest of the crowd. Once inside the church, the padre delivered the grand mass and sprinkled the new alcaldes with holy water. Later in a private meeting with the new alcaldes and Maya officials, the padre told the latter that, "although they were great in respect to the other Indians, yet in respect to the principal alcaldes they were but small men."[18] Stephens's account portrays with vividness the new power dynamics in which Maya officials appeared as secondary figures to the more important non-indigenous alcaldes.

Ascending to his post of cacique in a community exhausted by cholera, Canché probably did not experience the fanfare of inauguration such as Stephens witnessed in Nohcacab. But in other ways his experience would have shown him that in the eyes of the state he was still a "small man" compared to the local officials such as alcaldes. Despite being "small men," however, many caciques would quickly learn to take advantage of the incursion of local civil officials by engaging in strategic alliance making. The life of Macedonio Dzul of Peto provides an example.

In December 1829, Dzul requested to be reinstated to the office of cacique, a post he had previously renounced to escape the abuses of the subdelegado Antonio Gutiérrez.[19] On 31 December 1831, the order arrived from Mérida to return Dzul his charge as cacique of Peto. Despite this seemingly happy ending, however, Dzul's travails were by no means over. Five years after his reinstatement, in November 1836, Dzul once again became a victim of abuse at the hands of local state officials. The subdelegado and juez of the town attacked him, seizing grain from his milpa and demanding money.[20] Yet Dzul was more than a victim of abuse at the hands of local civil authorities. Rather, over the course of the 1830s and 1840s he transformed himself into something of a political figure in the town of Peto. In 1832 he was one of the electors present in the town hall under the aegis of alcalde Faustino Gamboa to elect the three men who would travel to Mérida to take part in the coming election of the deputies of the Congreso General.[21] In 1843 he was one of the main Maya signatories to the plebiscite that reunified Yucatán with Mexico.[22]

Still, Dzul's political activities were not without controversy. By 1841 he was already at the center of a political maelstrom in Peto, where he was implicated in electoral fraud and accused of using coercive methods to force peasants to vote for particular candidates in municipal elections.[23] Dzul's increasing politicization was also reflected in his local relations. By the 1840s he had forged a political alliance with an influential creole and local government official, the alcalde primero Don Cornelio Souza. Together, Dzul and Souza would become prominent players in local politics even to the extent of eliciting fear among their political opponents over their influence on municipal elections.[24] For Macedonio Dzul, political influence would also translate to economic solvency, with the cacique becoming one of the wealthiest men in Peto by the mid-1850s.[25]

The lives of caciques such as Dzul highlight the increasing politicization of caciques in post-independence Yucatán. This process of politicization was not simply an accident of individual life histories but an expression of broader structural tendencies at work. Liberal ideology undergirded the policies of post-independence Latin American governments such as Mexico's. Liberalism with its ideology of equality was fundamentally opposed to the república system as well as to special privileges traditionally enjoyed by caciques. At the same time, however, liberal governments in the early national period recognized that economic productivity (another liberal goal) demanded the subjugation of indigenous people. This contradictory character of liberalism in Yucatán affected caciques, who by the 1820s were stripped of their traditional privileges yet allowed to exist as caciques in order to facilitate economic goals of tax collection and recruitment of labor. Macedonio Dzul's mistreatment at the hands of subdelegado Antonio Gutiérrez cannot be understood simply as personal enmity but rather as a result of structural tendencies at work in the 1820s, which progressively made the cacique powerless.

Ironically, it was this very powerlessness that intensified the cacique's politicization. The municipal revolution brought about by the establishment of nonindigenous ayuntamientos in the post-independence period had heightened the presence of government officials at the local level. As the cacique's official role became proscribed and his traditional privileges and legitimacy eroded, he increasingly sought strategic political alliances with powerful local figures including government officials in order to hold onto power at the local level. This was the case with Dzul. By becoming a political figure in Peto, he was able to establish himself as a powerful and wealthy cacique. The municipal revolution, which brought about ayuntamientos and their accompanying local government officials, was a vital factor in the intensifying politicization of caciques.

ALLIANCE MAKING

Documents from the post-independence period, and especially cases of *abusos de autoridad* (abuses of authority), show a plethora of ways in which caciques and local government officials interacted on the ground. It is important to recognize that such cases were a direct result of the appropriation of liberal language and ideals at the local level. Throughout the colonial period, government officials had engaged in abusive practices such as forced labor, whipping, and imprisonment. But the liberal ideology of the early national period provided the local population with a language that represented these habitual transgressions as illegal and as infringements on the rights of citizens that liberal ideals were supposed to safeguard.[26] The consequent proliferation of cases recorded as "abusos de autoridad" provides a rich source base for the examination of local politics in early national Yucatán.

Once installed new alcaldes and jueces de paz often acted as local tyrants. Indeed, numerous cases of "abusos de autoridad" serve to highlight the power these men wielded in Yucatecan villages and the fear that they inspired in its inhabitants, both indigenous and white. In 1832, for instance, Pablo Pérez, a nonindigenous resident of Cauich, complained that the alcalde Joaquín Anguas had imprisoned him and his wife.[27] In the same year, Juan Antonio Keb and several other indigenous persons from the barrios of San Mateo and Santa Barbara of Nohcacab complained against their alcalde, Luciano Negrón, for depriving them of their food rations and beating them up on false allegations of drunkenness.[28] In Kancabdzonot, both alcaldes Baltazar Baeza and José Ceferino Loria were implicated in abuse of authority. Baeza was accused of unjustly imprisoning a nonindigenous resident named Juan Lara, and the brother of José Ceferino, Felipe Loria, was alleged to be seizing money, chickens, and livestock from the residents of the pueblo with impunity. The internal alliances among alcaldes become apparent in that Baeza would turn a blind eye to Felipe's misdemeanors since he was José Ceferino's brother.[29] The unpopularity of many alcaldes can be seen in the fact that, irrespective of race, residents of pueblos felt violated by their alcaldes. For instance, both nonindigenous and indigenous residents of the pueblo of Cantamayec in the *partido* (district) of Sotuta complained against their alcalde, Benito Fuentes, accusing him of, among other things, drunkenness, bribery, and corruption.[30]

Despite the unpopularity of certain local officials, the power they wielded made them potent allies for caciques. In the towns of Tabi and Tibolón, the alcalde, José Manuel Avilés, became universally unpopular because of the heavy-handed way in which he dealt with the townspeople. In 1832 testimonies revealed that 120 indígenas had emigrated out of Tabi to escape the abuses of this alcalde. What is striking is that, despite the near universal belief among the townspeople of the alcalde's culpability, the cacique testified on his behalf. The cacique asserted that the alcalde had never abused the residents of the town and that, although it was true that 120 indígenas had left the town, they had done so freely and voluntarily to avoid religious and civil taxes.[31]

In an area such as Yucatán, which lacked natural mineral resources and exceptionally fertile land, the labor of the numerous Maya residents became one of the only profitable resources that the area could offer. Caciques often proved critical allies to government officials in recruiting and redirecting labor, in some cases to the detriment of the indigenous communities. In 1831 in Quelul, the cacique Dionisio Collí supported the juez de paz, who forced indígenas to labor in distant fields and also imprisoned two officers of the indigenous república. In return the juez backed the cacique's authority in república matters.[32] In 1829, Juan Ignacio Aké and his other *compañeros* of the pueblo of

Petutillo complained about the cacique of the pueblo for colluding with the subdelegado and forcing them to work without pay in the fields of the government official.[33]

A particularly instructive case comes from the town of Cholul, where indígenas Manuel Canché, Bernardino Canché, Bernardo Catzim, José María Puc, and Manuel Akil complained that their juez de paz, Enrique Gonzáles, was forcing them to work on his property as well as that of the subdelegado and the *cura* (parish priest) of the town. Not only had the juez forced indígenas to work on the fields of the different town authorities, but he had also forced two *semaneros* (lit. weekly laborers) to work for him making sacks of henequen. This had created a problem in the community, since the semaneros had been unable to work in the community fields.[34] Since most of the local authorities from the juez to the subdelegado and even the cura owned substantial property, directing labor to these properties became a primary cause of "abusos de autoridad." And in this endeavor, the cacique presented himself as a vital ally.

In this case of Cholul, the cacique was an integral component of the network of power comprising the juez and the other local officials. Testimonies from the case reveal that the cacique acted as the intermediary between the juez and the indigenous workers and tried to recruit them to work on the lands of the government officials. The juez had even given the cacique money to distribute to the workers during recruitment at the rate of a half-real per *mecate* of land to be cultivated.[35] Nevertheless, the Cholul cacique was not simply an intermediary caught in the middle; he exercised his own power in order to aid and abet the juez. For instance, when the indigenous men resisted his attempts at labor recruitment, the cacique put them in prison.

We can also find evidence of local government officials using their alliance with caciques for personal gain. The case of Andrés Maldonado, juez de paz of the pueblo of Muna, is an apt example. In 1831 a Maya man named Pedro Euán complained that the juez had tried to prevent him from marrying a woman named Tomasa Poot. In his endeavor to prevent this union, the juez had gone to the extent of capturing Poot and then sending her to the house of one Felipe. On learning about Euán's allegations, Maldonado claimed that he had adopted Poot as a child and brought her up as his own daughter; he had sent her for a few days to the house of Felipe (who appears to have been a close associate of Maldonado) to protect her from Euán's overtures. Though Maldonado's own account of these events paints him as a protective father, historians have pointed out that "adoption" and god-parentage (*compadrazgo*) were often euphemisms for master-servant relationships.[36] There are numerous cases all through the nineteenth century of children being "adopted" by officials and commercial land owners and made to be laborers on plantations or household servants. In any event, as the case unfolds we find allegations that the cacique of the pueblo was complicit with the juez to the extent of forcing Euán to sign false testimonies that would favor the juez.[37] This case suggests that the cacique was closely allied with the juez even to the extent of supporting him in his own personal matters. It also shows that for the juez the cacique was a valuable ally. As a community head, the cacique had a certain degree of influence in local politics. He could resolve an issue in the juez's favor with simply the stroke of a pen—in this case by concocting a false testimony.

Of course, as caciques responded to the new local dynamic by allying with powerful local officials they were also normalizing political conduct based on clientelism. In this process a new kind of cacique was emerging, one that looked to Hispanic officials rather than the indigenous community for legitimacy. The case of Propocio Cocom of Pich is a useful example. This cacique, who was known for shackling and imprisoning villagers, whipping them, seizing their animals, and demanding double the required taxes, relied on both force and strategic alliances to remain in power. Cocom derived his power in large part from his strategic alliance with the local alcalde, Peón. When indígenas tired of the cacique's mistreatment went to their alcalde to complain against the cacique, rather than help them he brought them back to Cocom. Alliance with Peón also afforded Cocom an additional advantage: he was able to count on the allegiance of the local military force to undergird his power.

Traditionally, local Maya constables, or *tupiles*, as they had been known, had supplemented the cacique and the república as the police arm of the indigenous council. With the incursion of government officials, including law enforcement officials, in towns and villages, documents in the early national period show a disappearance of the tupiles from local law enforcement. Instead, government-appointed soldiers stationed in pueblos or cantons were sometimes called upon by alcaldes whenever they needed a show of force. This can be seen, for instance, in the pueblo of Ebtún, where the alcalde auxiliar sent three soldiers to punish an indigenous man, Marcelo Un, for not paying religious taxes. Un was whipped by the soldiers and then imprisoned.[38] When soldiers passed through a locality, caciques were called upon to provide food and supplies, including mules to carry their belongings and arms. Failure to comply could result in punishment. This was the case for the cacique of San Antonio Sahcabchén, who was imprisoned for not providing enough beasts of burden when a troop passed through his pueblo.[39] A cacique could also count on the help of these military men, especially if he was in league with the local alcalde.

In this Pich case, the cacique Cocom's strategic alliance with the local alcalde allowed him to take advantage of *soldados cívicos* (civil soldiers) to terrorize the village. On his order the soldiers imprisoned the complaining indígenas and then extracted money from them. Cocom continued to abuse villagers with impunity, and his local network of alliances help explain why it took almost another two years before he was finally removed from his post.[40] By himself a cacique may not have been all-powerful. But through complicity and alliance with a government official such as an alcalde he could reign as a veritable despot. This was essentially what had happened with Propocio Cocom of Pich.

Antagonistic relations between a cacique and other local officials often meant the end of the cacique's career. This was the case in Dzitbalché, where the cacique was removed from office because he refused to put up with the mistreatment of the indígenas by the alcalde and cura of the town.[41] In Tepich, the cacique Bautista Canul was arraigned and held in police custody for illegally trying to raise money from community members, which he intended to send to the governor in order to effect the removal of taxes in his community. In his testimony the cacique maintained his innocence and explained that his only fault had been his inability to answer the summons of the alcaldes ordering him to wash and clean the streets and the plaza.[42]

Certain government officials also seemed to have a greater degree of animosity toward caciques than others. Antonio Gutiérrez, the subdelegado responsible for the dismissal of Macedonio Dzul from office in the 1820s, also oversaw at least two other cases in 1829 that led to the dismissal of caciques.[43] When Norberto Dzib, an indigenous resident of the pueblo of Cantamayec, complained about the cacique of that pueblo, the government asked the alcalde of the town to draw up a summary of the case and then send it to the juez for final resolution.[44] It is not hard to see that, since caciques were officially accountable to government officials, allying with these men could mean the difference between survival as cacique or removal from office.

Economic developments over the course of the early national period further complicated the power dynamics on the ground. The early national period in Yucatán saw the burgeoning of *haciendas* (commercial plantations) following the Constitution of 1825, which established the goal of privatizing land and using it for commercial purposes.[45] The rise of haciendas threatened indigenous communal resources, often putting the interests of *hacendados* (owners of the haciendas) and indígenas at cross-purposes. Struggles over land and resources occurred all over the peninsula, as in the pueblo of Sabancuy, where indigenous and private interests struggled over rights to land to raise livestock.[46] And because there were now local government officials at the village level, these conflicts were not just between communities and hacendados but rather were more complex sites of struggle. Caciques frequently came into direct contact with hacendados, who, for example, were often responsible for paying the taxes owed by their servants.[47]

A case from the pueblo of Acanceh in 1828 shows the intertwining of local figures in power struggles on the ground. Here an indígena, Hermenegildo Canul, and hacendado, Manuel Antonio Castellanos (owner of hacienda Venecla), came into conflict over the ownership of some cattle. Castellanos claimed that when he was absent from the town Canul had stolen three of his *novillos* (young bulls). The alcalde of the town ruled that the novillos belonged to Canul. Castellanos argued that the alcalde should have waited for his return before making such a decision. Additionally, Castellanos claimed that three of his servants were put in prison later on false charges of robbing

Canul of twelve pesos. According to Castellanos, not only were the allegations against his servants untrue, but the alcalde's actions were infringements of Castellanos's constitutional rights. He asked that the alcalde be deposed.

This case seems to involve the landholder and the alcalde, but closer inspection reveals that the cacique of the town played a vital role in precipitating this conflict. Testimonies in the case reveal that the cacique of Tekit had ordered two men to go to the *sitio* Pachtel because he believed that Canul was harboring vagrants in it.[48] The practice of vagrancy had been the bane of governments ever since the colonial times. Of course, what the government termed "vagrancy" and labeled as idleness was actually the long-standing practice of Maya peasants leaving their pueblos in search of lands to cultivate. Often this involved going to the *montes* (bush) and clearing a small plot of land for growing corn. Wishing to control the peasant population (and, consequently, extract taxes and labor from them), the government cast this traditional practice as vagrancy. For example, one of the declared reasons for the reinstatement of indigenous repúblicas in 1824 was "to contain the dispersion of the indígenas in the forests and find them an honest occupation that makes them useful to society."[49] Indeed, one of the cacique's duties was to control this dispersion of population.

It was such a search for vagrants that brought the cacique of Tekit into the struggle between Canul and Castellanos. The cacique suspected that Canul was harboring vagrants in his sitio. To facilitate the search, the cacique ordered his men to seek help from the servants of hacienda Venecla, since it was close to the sitio, and three servants joined in the hunt. When they arrived at the sitio, the only thing the servants could find were a basket with some old clothes, some beans, and an old handkerchief; Canul had helped the indígenas escape. Apparently Canul also got in touch with the alcalde and alleged that the three servants of hacienda Venecla had come to his property and stolen twelve pesos from him. Without investigating, the alcalde Manrique put the three servants in jail. Castellanos now demanded that the alcalde be deposed for his illegal behavior.[50]

In this case the alcalde appears to have acted in the interests of the indígena Canul against the hacendado Castellanos. We do not know why the alcalde acted this way, but we do know that personal economic interests often played a role in the decisions of local officials. This was, for instance, what happened in the pueblo of Ucú when the juez de paz supported villagers against the hacendado Felipe Gil, who wanted to acquire *baldío* (fallow) lands to establish a cattle ranch. In this case the juez was part of the creole landowning class of Ucú and saw Gil's designs as a threat to his own properties.[51] Whatever the reasons may have been in the alcalde Manrique's case, it is clear that the very presence in the pueblos of government officials changed the balance of power at the local level. At the same time, the presence of caciques influenced local power dynamics. Through their function as controllers of vagrancy, caciques proved to be a key variable in the local power struggles involving hacendados, indígenas, and local government officials—in this case, the alcalde.[52]

Government officials and hacendados were powerful at the local level, and alliance with them could certainly augment a cacique's power. At the same time, caciques themselves could be powerful forces, especially if they retained the support of their communities. In Nohcacab, for instance, during the 1820s a communally built well (*pozo*) passed into the hands of hacendados who began to charge rent from the indigenous community to use it. In this case, after almost twenty years of struggle over the water resource, the cacique Apolonio Che and other members of the indigenous república were able to promote litigation against the hacendados and recover their right to use the pozo.[53] Similarly, as representatives of their communities caciques also sometimes resisted the designs of local government officials. We can see instances of this in the petitions forwarded by indigenous residents of towns against local government officials. For instance, when residents of Cantamayec complained about the alcalde Benito Fuentes for various abuses, the cacique was among the indigenous people who provided testimony against the alcalde.[54] The presence of a document in Mayan signed by the cacique in the petition forwarded by Juan Antonio Keb and other indígenas against the alcalde Luciano Negrón of Nohcacab suggests that they received support from the cacique for the petition.[55] When their subdelegado began to collect taxes from the villagers of Tecoh with unprecedented rigor, violently imprisoning villagers, it was the cacique together with the república members of Tecoh who complained to the governor.[56] These examples complicate the picture of cacique relations with powerful local figures and provide a useful counterpoint to the view that caciques universally sought to gain local power at the expense of their communities.

THE COMMUNITY AS SOURCE OF CACIQUE POWER

Understandably, communities everywhere in Yucatán resented the intervention of state officials in the years after independence, and complaints against overbearing officials were common. In the town of Kaua, for instance, the cacique and other indígenas complained of mistreatment at the hand of their alcalde, who they claimed had come to his post because of his connections to important people in the town.[57] Similarly, in 1841 the cacique of Dzitnup, José Sabino Pat, traveled to Mérida with other indígenas to petition the government for the removal of their alcalde auxiliar.[58] Cenotillo too saw a backlash against its alcalde, although Andrés Canché was not directly involved in it. While Canché was being arraigned for his involvement in embezzlement of public funds, on 10 May 1836 several disgruntled Maya led by one Pablo Dzin raised complaints against the alcalde Barrera, who had been responsible for Canché's removal.[59] Canché remained uninvolved in these complaints, but it is not hard to imagine that Maya of his community viewed his firing as yet another attack on their own autonomy. A year after being replaced, Canché still considered himself a community leader and "cacique of Cenotillo."[60]

Various documentary evidence from the 1820–40 period suggests caciques sometimes abused their authority in relation to their communities. As noted earlier, the cacique Bautista Canul asked the community members to give him money and livestock with which to bribe the governor and remove a tax. And cases of abuse were not limited to extracting money from villagers. The archives record numerous cases of cacique drunkenness and of whipping and imprisoning indigenous residents. The cacique of Tela, for instance, was known to whip indígenas regularly and imprison them at whim, releasing them only when he so desired.[61]

In some cases such behavior briefly established the cacique's authority, but it also brought him into conflict with the community, the very entity that was supposed to be the bulwark of his power. Alienating other república officers in particular made the cacique more vulnerable. The cacique and the other members of the indigenous república such as *tenientes* (deputies) and regidores did not always see eye to eye. The cacique of Tahdziú, for instance, not only neglected his duty through drunkenness but also put the teniente in prison.[62] Abusing other indígenas, and especially república officers, could open the way for a cacique's rapid demise. One example comes from the pueblo of Chichanhá, where the república and indigenous residents of the town denounced to the governor their cacique, Dámaso Ye, who had for more than six years abused them.[63] Similar denunciations of caciques and their subsequent dismissals serve to emphasize that muscle power could boost the cacique for only so long.

Ultimately, caciques still depended on their communities for legitimacy. This explains why one of the first actions local officials took against caciques whom they wished to remove was to beat and humiliate them in front of their república members and community.[64] It was not being appointed by the government that legitimated a cacique as the indigenous leader in the eyes of his people; it was his long history of association with the community. Nowhere is this clearer than in the case of Sambula. The pueblo of Sambula was separated from the jurisdiction of Lerma on 2 October 1830 by the superior decree of the governor. After this date, the pueblo was made a *sujeto* (subject, both economic and governmental) of the pueblo of San Roman. The Sambula indígenas were now under the cacique of San Roman—but they never recognized him as their legitimate cacique. Rather, they asked to be returned to the jurisdiction of Lerma.[65]

An interesting aspect of this case is that it was the teniente de cura of the pueblo of Sambula who acted as a protector against the abuses of the cacique, and he was also the key figure in helping the indígenas petition against the cacique. Again we see how the long history of communities shaped their relationships to caciques. The community alleged that the cacique was sending its people to the *salinas* (salt mine) to work against their wishes. In response the alcalde of Campeche,

Juan Antonio Ramírez, supported the cacique, saying that after a thorough investigation he had found that the cacique of San Roman had done exactly what he had been told to do, giving the right proportion of indígenas in the population the task of going to the salinas. It was the same proportion other barrios had contributed to the work. Ramírez also asserted that salt mining was the best and most important source of *riqueza* (riches) for the state, and that working the mines had always been accepted among the population and resulted in the common good. In this case the community and the teniente de cura pitted themselves against the cacique and the alcalde. What was determinative in this case was the community's view of its own history. The community did not recognize the cacique of San Roman as legitimate because he had not traditionally been part of their community but rather had been imposed on them by the government.

Conversely, allegiance to the community could form the basis of power and legitimacy for the cacique. This clearly comes through in the case of Don Mauricio May, cacique of Xocén. During his tenure May had been subject to humiliation and punishment by the alcalde auxiliar, Santiago de la Cruz Pérez, and later by the alcalde, Teodoro Pérez. On one occasion he had even been shackled and imprisoned for eight days.[66] In 1839, May traveled to Mérida to present to the governor a petition against the cura of Xocén, Juan de Dios Helguera, and his minister, Juan Pablo Escalante. In his declaration May wrote that as head (*cabeza*) of the pueblo he had come with several residents of Xocén to present their grievances to the governor. This declaration reveals many interesting features. He clearly did not see himself as a functionary, but rather as a political head of the town. We also learn that the cura and the local government officials were in alliance; the cura had denounced the indígenas of the town as shameless and without respect for the jueces de paz.[67] May's petition posed a threat to the local church and government officials, which likely explains why he was suspended from office soon after.

Yet May's career as a cacique did not end here. He continued to act as the village head and returned to Mérida in January 1841 again to complain to the governor, this time against the alcaldes of the town. In his petition, the suspended cacique charged the alcalde, Santiago de la Cruz Pérez, along with the subdelegado of the partido, for maltreatment of the indígenas of the pueblo.[68] Many residents of the pueblo backed him up with their own testimonies, once again showing a community that did not see the cacique as the government saw him—a functionary whose main job was to collect taxes. Rather, May was seen as a legitimate leader whose power came from his long association with and allegiance to the community.

Like Macedonio Dzul or Propocio Cocom, Mauricio May gives us a story of politicization. Like them, May's process of politicization was influenced by his interactions with local government and church officials. However, the nature of this politicization was different: it was the suffering and harassment that he and his community experienced at the hands of local officials that politicized May. Unlike Dzul and Cocom, May drew his power and legitimacy from his allegiance to his community rather than alliances with local officials. His process of politicization thus occurred not through alliances with officials but rather through a rejection of them. For Dzul and Cocom, it was the official status as cacique that made them useful allies to local officials and guaranteed their power. It is unlikely that they would retain any such power after their terms as cacique were over. In contrast, legitimacy in the eyes of community gave May the ability to act as a political headman even when he was no longer a cacique and ensured his persistence as a local authority figure. By the end of the 1830s, therefore, May had espoused an alternative mode of politicization—one that relied on allegiance with the community rather than alliance with local officials to exercise power.

In general, the official status of caciques declined over the early national period. In the eyes of the post-independence government, caciques now were not much more than simple tax collectors. Yet archival documents from the 1820s to the early 1840s suggest a parallel process of intensifying politicization. A close reading of these documents suggests that caciques constituted powerful, even political, figures in their respective localities. Men such as Macedonio Dzul did not exist as apolitical functionaries but were intrinsically involved in the political life of the pueblos. Moreover, these caciques did not act in a vacuum. Rather, cacique politics was an outcome of complex relationships at the local level. The cacique drew his power from the relationships he forged at the local level with local government officials, ecclesiastical and military authorities, and the community he represented. What seems apparent is that faced with a new set of rules and institutions that formally excluded them from power, caciques began to forge what can only be termed as clientelist relations with local authority figures. Over time this sort of private politicking would become the modus operandi of cacique politics.

Caciques who would become vanguards of the Caste War such as Jacinto Pat also experienced power plays at the local level. In 1838–39, for instance, Pat was involved in a legal battle against the juez of Tihosuco, Perfecto Bolis.[69] What is clear is the overwhelming evidence of the importance of local relations in shaping cacique politics. There was no indication yet of the violent turn these political power struggles would take. This would become evident in the later 1840s with the emergence of the rebellion, when caciques such as Pat and Cecilio Chí would embrace Mauricio May's kind of alternative politicization and go to battle in defense of their communities.

CHAPTER 3

For God, Glory, and Taxes

Caciques and the Politics of Taxation on the Eve of Yucatán's Caste War

In 1837, a year after being removed from office, Andrés Canché sent a petition to the governor denying allegations that he had embezzled money collected as taxes from the residents of Cenotillo. He attributed the misunderstanding to the actions of the subdelegado of Valladolid, Manuel Elizalde.[1] Because he was ill, Canché explained, he had sent the money with his scribe, Feliciano Couoh, to the subdelegado. Elizalde then claimed that fourteen pesos were missing, seized four of Canché's horses, and removed him from the post of cacique.

Manuel Elizalde wasted no time in responding to these accusations. On 10 April 1837 he wrote to the governor denying the cacique's allegations.[2] Yes, Canché and Couoh had been removed from office, as the law prescribed, declared unfit to serve for a period of three years, and ordered to pay the amount defrauded as well as the costs of the case. Elizalde further asserted that when the two men were declared insolvent, not only had he not forced them to work to generate the money (*vendido al trabajo*), as had been ordered during their dismissal, but he had used his own money to pay the *hacienda pública* the fourteen pesos. Angry and slandered, Elizalde urged the governor to punish this "indígena" for his vile accusations.

This case reveals the undercurrents of distrust and tension that mired towns and villages of Yucatán in the post-independence period. Sifting through archival documents from these years, one is struck by the recurrence of the same motif: the cacique and escribano dismissed on charges of embezzlement of taxes. In 1838, Eusebio May, cacique of Nohcacab, and his scribe, Victoriano Chan, were charged with embezzling the money they had collected as taxes from the pueblo and their properties were to be expropriated to cover for the money embezzled.[3] Similarly in 1842, the cacique Patricio Poot of Ebtún and his escribano were charged with embezzling public money.[4]

Even though municipalization had been instituted with the intention of streamlining administrative processes, in reality the new order of things settled uneasily in the minds of both Hispanics and Maya in the early national period. Now that both vecinos and indígenas had to work together to administer the pueblos, the cracks in the new municipal system seemed to become more visible. Interestingly, the residents Canché was accused of cheating were vecinos who had paid taxes for themselves and their indigenous servants. And when Elizalde responded to Canché's allegations, he emphasized that it was the indígena Canché who was in the wrong. The undercurrent of racial tension is clear in these documents despite the fact that the language of legality appears to represent the matter as a purely fiscal one.

In the years leading up to the Caste War, tax collection would become central to cacique politics at the local level. Arguments over the onerous church tax (*obvención*), in particular, would be the spark that led to the all-out conflagration of 1847. In that violent rebellion, some of the first flashes of trouble would be in towns with a history of resistance to taxation.

THE POLITICS OF TAX COLLECTION

Though in the early national period, especially with the onset of ayuntamientos, the cacique's role became increasingly restricted, one function that continued to be assigned to the cacique was tax collection. The failure of using government officials to collect taxes during the brief periods when the república was abolished in the early 1800s had conveyed to the government the importance of using indigenous mechanisms. In fact, a primary reason for the reinstatement of repúblicas and caciques was to facilitate the collection of taxes. This motive is obvious in the May 1824 declaration of Yucatán's congress: "That for the collection of the established taxes, and only for this objective, respecting the indígenas, the old repúblicas de indios should be reestablished."[5] The government tried to ensure the viability of this system by always electing caciques who were financially well off. Not only would a wealthy cacique have less reason to stoop to corruption, but in the event that a cacique did embezzle money his assets could be seized. Indeed, in some documents concerning cacique elections, authorities spelled this out as a qualification. In 1831, for example, the cacique of Hunucma was chosen because he had enough wealth to cover any losses.[6] Manuel Elizalde was thus following a long-established custom when he seized Andrés Canché's assets.

Even though the government regarded caciques as mere functionaries who would aid in tax collection, closer examination reveals that even this function was essentially political in nature. On a fundamental level, the very fact that they were tax collectors gave caciques a great deal of power and even impunity. To start with, caciques were allowed to keep a small portion of the taxes collected as a salary.[7] Moreover, his role as tax collector allowed the cacique to exercise power and even force against his community. This can be clearly seen in the case of the barrio of San Cristóbal in Mérida, where residents Sebastián and Manuel May complained that their cacique raided their house at midnight and put them in prison, all in order to collect the personal tax. In this case, the cacique had raided the men's home with the complicity of other local government officials. He appears to have consulted the alcalde segundo, Félix Fajardo, who advised him to imprison the debtors. The members of the ayuntamiento also wrote to the governor supporting the cacique's actions.[8] It is easy to imagine that, given such alliances and a sanction to mete out punishment as he saw fit, the cacique could quite easily become a powerful figure in the local community.

Nevertheless, it would be a mistake to assume that communities simply gave in to tax demands without a fight. This can be seen in the case of indígena Juan de Mata Cocom, who tried to incite the indígenas of Timucuy to resist paying the civil and ecclesiastical taxes to the cacique and alcalde. Cocom was something of a political figure who was once arraigned for gathering a multitude of indígenas in his house with a plan to influence municipal voting.[9] Resistance to tax collection also came in passive forms; fleeing from pueblos because of heavy tax loads was a perennial response of poverty-stricken indigenous residents.[10] The república itself could disagree with a cacique and try to resist taxation, as was the case in Seyé, where the república members (with the notable exception of the cacique) asked the government to let them delay payment of the personal tax.[11] Tax collection was thus a constant site of struggle in the indigenous community.

Struggles over tax collection can also be viewed as moments in local political struggle. Since the cacique's legitimacy in the eyes of the government now depended on efficient tax collection, his rivals or enemies could use the discourse on taxation to undermine his power. This was likely the case in the pueblo of Dzitbalché. Here, the cacique was removed apparently because of his apathy to collecting obvenciones. However, the república members maintained that this had been merely a pretext to remove the cacique. They claimed that the indígenas of the pueblo were abused by their alcalde and the cura, and it was the cacique's opposition to these abusive officials and his desire to protect the community from them that had resulted in his being ousted.[12]

Another case, this one from the town of Yaxcabá, similarly shows how local political struggles became superimposed on the question of tax collection. In 1827 the cacique of Yaxcabá, Lázaro Camal, was dismissed from his position after it surfaced that he was absent from his duties and inept at collecting taxes. Though it was the alcalde concilidador who sent the petition for the dismissal of the cacique, the testimonies in the case reveal that an informer had denounced the cacique, which led the alcalde to remove him. An indígena named Juan Pablo Camal had complained that he and his companions had gone to the house of Lázaro Camal to pay their taxes and found that he was absent.[13] Juan Pablo Camal was himself the longtime cacique of Kancabdzonot, a small pueblo in the parish of Yaxcabá.[14] As a cacique himself, Camal was a respected figure in local society and his words would have had particular weight with the alcalde conciliador. It is possible that local rivalry between the two caciques expressed itself in this case. As in Dzitbalché, the Yaxcabá case serves to illustrate how local power struggles colored the seemingly routine act of tax collection.

CACIQUES, CHURCH OFFICIALS, AND THE OBVENCIÓN

Although the conquest of Latin America had been as much for "God" as for gold and glory, and priests, or curas, had been the cornerstone of the colonization process, by the end of the colonial period they had begun losing much of their power. In Yucatán, as in the rest of Spanish America, in the period following first the Bourbon reforms and then the Constitution of Cádiz of 1812 there was a progressive decline in the status of curas. This reduction in power, which continued into the early national period, made local politics and strategic alliances all the more important to curas if they were to survive with their power intact. Cacique relations with curas reflect the interdependence each side relied on to maintain local power.

The Constitution of 1812 created an atmosphere of almost millenarian expectations among indigenous populations. Indeed, as Ceferino Domínguez, alcalde of Nohcacab complained, indígenas of the town were refusing to "hear mass, confess or pay church fees."[15] The cura of Uayma, Fray Pablo Guzmán, complained that children had ceased coming to the school of *primeras letras* (primary school), and there was great opposition to learning Christian doctrine and letters. Moreover, according to the Guzmán, the indígenas now resisted doing any service for the church.[16] Documents from this period show similar conflicts between church and indigenous populations in other parts of Yucatán. In the pueblo of Tinum in 1813, the cacique and members of the indigenous república complained to the Diputación Provincial of Yucatán against their cura, Pablo Carrillo.[17] The cacique alleged that the cura had beaten up and imprisoned young children because they had been unable to give him the usual *higuerilla y huevos*—castor oil and eggs. In response to the cacique's complaints, the alcalde came to the cura's defense, explaining that he was distressed over the behavior of the indigenous people of the town. For not only had the children of the village stopped coming to Sunday school, but there were other offenses against God: only one person in the pueblo had recently gotten married; the others were living in sin. Similarly, in 1820 the cura of Sotuta, Francisco Ángel López, noted that his congregation no longer came to the church gate to receive instruction, as was customary.[18]

The nonattendance at Sunday school and disinclination to marry were not simply anathema to the cura for religious reasons; they also meant that a longtime stable source of church income was now under attack. For just as attendance in school required the fee of oil and eggs, other religious rituals such as baptism, marriage, and burial had always come with a fee to the cura. By attacking this source of income, the villagers were threatening the power of the church authorities in the locality. It is interesting to note that in the Tinum case, a conflict between the cura and the república led by the cacique, the alcalde sided with the cura. As we see below, this was not the only way the network of power in the local level operated. Rather, as the careers of curas and caciques both came increasingly under threat in the early national period, caciques and curas even made common cause.

Under the national government, the obvención remained the most important source of financial solvency for the church. It was an annual head tax of twelve and a half reales for men and nine reales for women, a considerable sum at the time. The revenues from this tax were so great that obvenciones together with other church taxes helped individual parishes acquire almost two thousand pesos annually.[19] It is thus not surprising that most of the cases involving priests and local authority figures arose from the collection of this tax. Under the early national government, in fact, the cacique was responsible for collecting not only the civil tax but also the obvención. Predictably, the cacique and cura crossed paths frequently. The cacique had perhaps the most intimate knowledge of the pueblo and its people of any local authority. Using this knowledge, the cacique drew up lists of the persons resident in the pueblo who would be taxed.[20] He also recruited workers to labor in the church, such as construction or repair of the church buildings.[21]

Collection of religious taxes strained relations among local authorities. The cura of Kopomá, for instance, accused the juez de paz of the pueblo of preventing indígenas from paying burial fees. Testimonies including those of república members of the town reveal that monetary hardship was preventing the residents from paying their fees, and that the juez had nothing to do with it.[22] Here, even though there was no proof of juez involvement, the cura saw him as the primary rival in local society.

Collection of obvenciones had the potential to spark both conflict and alliances among local authorities, thus influencing the local power struggle in each pueblo. In the pueblo of Baca, collection of obvenciones pit the cacique against the subdelegado. During the early 1820s, Baca faced a crisis of food. Shortage of grain afflicted the community and led many indígenas to migrate to other places. By 1831, when many of these immigrants started returning to Baca, the cura asked them to pay the obvenciones for the years they had been missing from the pueblo. The cacique decried the cura's actions, but the subdelegado Manuel Ponce supported the cura, who he said had not only collected less tax than he was owed but had also offered to receive the debt in installments depending on individual circumstances.[23] Other documents from the period show curas understanding the need to maintain relations of alliance with the indigenous communities. For instance, during a shortage of grain in the ranchos of Chac and Kauil, *anexos* (dependencies) of the pueblo of Nohcacab, the cura let the indigenous residents pay their taxes in a way that they would be able to meet. In contrast, the juez de paz of the pueblo attempted to extract tribute through harsh means.[24]

Collection of obvenciones was certainly a sticky issue, but relations between cura and cacique meant more than efficient tax collection. At the local level, relations between these two had direct consequences for their survival. This is poignantly conveyed in a fascinating case from Opichén.[25] In 1831 the subdelegado of the partido of Hunucmá ordered the priest, Presbitero Pedro José Montañez, to vacate the *casa de pósito* (storehouse intended for storing grain) that he had been occupying so that it could be rented out for two pesos a month to one Juan Mugartegui. Both the juez de paz and the subdelegado accused the priest of using the storehouse as a tavern and *carniceria* (butcher's shop), which was against public interests because the casa de pósito was near a prison and a public chapel. On 26 May 1831, Pedro Montañez asked the juez de paz to let him stay in the casa in exchange for a monthly fee equal to that offered by Mugartegui.

In this case, where two of the most powerful local officials, the juez and the subdelegado, were clearly against the priest, Montañez drew support from unlikely quarters—the cacique and república of Opichén. The república de indígenas, led by the cacique Andrés Balam, argued that the casa de pósito had been unused for some time. To put it to use, the república and local authorities had agreed to let the padre and his family stay in the casa. The república members asserted that Montañez had opened a school of primeras letras in the casa, where he was giving lessons without taking a fee; since he was the only teacher in the pueblo, it was in the interest of the community that he be allowed to remain.

This case attracted attention outside of Opichén as well. On 30 May, the *provisor* (purveyor) of the Church of Yucatán, José María Meneses, told the subdelegado and jefe político of Hunucmá that if Padre Montañez could pay the same rent as Mugartegui, then the preference should be given to the public official. Meneses emphasized that it was a time of great *inopia* (dearth, lack) for priests everywhere in Yucatán and that the government should try to help them. Under pressure from both the indigenous república and the provisor, the governor decided in favor of Montañez; the priest could stay in the casa if he agreed to pay two pesos monthly as rent and did not commit any "excesses" there.

This case is instructive on many levels. The provisor's statement serves to show the relative powerlessness and poverty of priests in the post-independence period. The discourse on education and the need for children—especially Maya children—to attend school was something that had been promulgated by the Diputación Provincial as well as the national government.[26] Indeed, the government had long held education to be a civilizing tool for indigenous people, and with independence it assumed an almost demagogical aspect.[27] The cacique in this case, Andrés Balam, in fact argued that the priest was providing free education and thus used this state rhetoric on education as a means of saving the priest from eviction.

The Opichén case shows the importance of a cacique to the survival of a cura, but the reverse also took place. An interesting case of cacique-cura interaction comes from the barrio of Santiago in Mérida. In 1831 a cacique named Marcelino Puch was arraigned on charges of conspiracy against the government, held, and then released on amnesty. While he was incarcerated, another indígena, Santiago Pacab, fulfilled the duties of cacique. During his brief tenure, Pacab seems to have forged an alliance with the cura of the parish of Santiago. It was probably Puch's release from prison that galvanized the cura into action. On 24 October 1831, the cura wrote to the governor that the interim cacique had been better at tax collection than Puch and that in the national interest Pacab should become the permanent cacique. Despite the cura's best efforts, however, Puch was reinstated in accordance with the decree of his amnesty.[28] In this case the cura was unable to help Pacab retain the position, though without the amnesty decree it is quite possible that he would have prevailed.

In general, then, after the Constitution of Cádiz disgruntled curas accused indígenas and their caciques of neglecting their duties toward the church. During the 1820s and '30s, however, curas and caciques came to recognize the importance of mutual alliances to retain their power in local society in face of the progressive erosion of their traditional prestige and privileges. That these alliances took place in spite of the divisive issue of the obvención is itself remarkable.

ORIGINS OF A LOCAL STRUGGLE

Local politics was not immune to wider developments at the regional and even national level. The post-independence period was a complex one filled with instability. There were repeated hostilities between federalists and centralists, liberals and conservatives. One of the most important episodes in nineteenth-century Yucatecan history was the revolt led by Santiago Imán. Historians see the Imán revolt as a turning point in Yucatecan history and a precursor to the Caste War—a long and bloody indigenous rebellion lasting from 1847 to 1901. Many now believe that a combination of pressures—economic, political, social, and even psychological—led the Maya peasantry to rise up in arms. Examination of cacique relations with local officials and curas in this period shows that as in the 1820s and 1830s there remained a great deal of interdependence between caciques and both other local officials and curas. Ultimately, however, it was the thorny issue of the obvención that exacerbated stresses at the local level.

In 1836 the Mexican government under General Santa Anna had abolished the federalist Constitution of 1824 and replaced it with the Siete Leyes (Seven Laws). This new Constitution of 1836 transformed the federal republic's states into military departments, which were governed by political bosses handpicked by Santa Anna.[29] Unsurprisingly, many of the former states chafed under the centralist yoke. In Yucatán, Santiago Imán, a military officer with a wealthy creole background, led a successful revolt against the centralist forces of Mexico, which at that time were embroiled in a war to reconquer Texas and needed men and arms from Yucatán. Imán's revolt brought Yucatán independence from Mexico for a brief period.[30] One of the key moments of the revolt was the declaration of the Act of Valladolid in February 1840, which held out the promise of abolition of the hated obvención. It is unarguable that the reason for Imán's decision to abolish these taxes was to gain the support of the Maya masses, who he hoped would join his military forces in the fight against Mexico. Imán's rebellion seems to have resonated in the small villages and towns that dotted the Yucatecan peninsula. Looking at the effects of the obvención law on local society provides a fascinating glimpse into how wider developments in regional politics on the eve of the Caste War affected local power nexuses.

Obvenciones had always been a bane of indigenous communities. Imán in his February 1840 declaration promised to abolish the obvenciones for both men and women and instead levy only a one real per month tax from indigenous men.[31] In the summer of 1840, the state congress confirmed the validity of Imán's Act of Valladolid and for the first time legally abolished obvenciones. The decree of 9 September 1840 announced that from 1 April 1840 obvenciones were to be replaced with a monthly religious tax of one real for males ages fourteen to sixty.[32] Article 3 of this decree instructed local authorities to collect this new tax as well as any obvenciones owed before that date. Regular civil taxes continued to be levied without change.

There was dissension among some indígenas, who had expected all taxes to be abolished. In the town of Ebtún the alcalde came into conflict with the indígenas when he ordered obvenciones due from January to March 1840 to be paid. The indígenas saw this as a violation of the promise made to them by Imán, and the resulting quarrel between the community and local officials led to resistance among indígenas, with some fleeing the pueblo to escape the taxes.[33]

The varied interpretations of Imán's declaration, including that it had abolished all religious taxation, spread like wildfire among the pueblos. In August 1840, Francisco Esquivel, alcalde primero of Ebtún, asserted that the "sinister" idea that indígenas were exempt from all taxes was spreading among the Maya.[34] Problems were compounded by the fact that caciques had traditionally received a percentage of taxes collected as salary, and it was thus in their interest to continue collecting these taxes even after they had been limited by law. But if they did, they faced backlash from indígenas.[35]

Aside from fleeing to avoid this tax collection,[36] in certain cases indígenas took more drastic action. The tensions created between caciques and their communities during this time can be seen in a case from the pueblo of Hopelchén. Here, in 1840, trouble started when the cacique Chan used violent measures to extract obvenciones from the indigenous residents. In response, almost two hundred indígenas under the leadership of one Tiburcio Mas gathered together to discuss how to remove Chan.[37] Local government authorities dispersed the gathering and charged the indígenas with rebellion and sedition, but this episode shows that struggles over taxes could take a political turn.

Surprisingly during this period, alcaldes also became involved in tax collection. This was an unprecedented occurrence and shows the desperation of the local authorities to extract taxes after the massive resistance generated by Imán's Act of Valladolid. The alcalde of Chemax, José María Rejón, generated dissent among the indígenas of rancho Jotoech by continuing to collect obvenciones despite the Act of Valladolid.[38] In collecting these taxes, alcaldes were dependent on the support of caciques. When Marcelo Un and other residents of Ebtún complained against their alcalde for collecting obvenciones, beating the indígenas, and seizing their chickens and livestock, it was the cacique who denied the accusations leveled against the alcalde.[39] The close alliance between caciques and alcaldes during this period can also be seen in the case of Cuzamá, where the alcalde tried to protect the cacique, who had collected obvenciones, from the ire of the resident indígenas.[40]

Despite the new obvención laws, the interdependence between local government officials and caciques built over the 1820s and '30s remained strong and the two entities continued to be entrenched in each other's political spheres in the early 1840s. As a result, indígenas and their caciques sometimes became tools for local jueces and bigmen to gain power in their political infighting. In December 1840, Pablo José Reyes, the alcalde of Calkiní, came into conflict with another influential resident, Pedro José Peña, over the parish elections. To resolve the dispute, the governor ordered a commission to produce a report about the crimes that Pedro José Peña had accused Reyes of perpetrating during the elections. Peña tried to manipulate the commission in his favor, coopting indigenous witnesses including the cacique.[41]

Along with caciques and local government officials, an important casualty of the new obvención law was the cura, who had long survived on the money collected from the religious taxes. In a way, the obvención had become the lifeblood of the church officials. Now the new obvención law threatened that source of livelihood too. The pressures that the cura found himself under and the consequences this had for his relationships with other important local figures comes through in a case from the parish of Peto. Here, in November 1840 the cura Joseph Sotero Brito expressed his anger over the fact that he had not received the fees for burials that should have been contributed to the parish. Brito pointed to the alcalde and subdelegado as the prime culprits for the penury of his church. He asserted that the obvención was now being collected by the subdelegado, and even though he had agreed to send a monthly installment of money to the cura, this had not happened. Given that new obvención laws had reduced church income, the cura was now more dependent on church fees such as those for burials. This too, the cura claimed, had been sabotaged by the alcalde, who had been preventing the residents of the pueblo from paying him burial fees. The alcalde Felipe Rosado replied that these allegations were completely false. He explained that some recent burials were those of very poor people. Since the cura would not do their burial rites without the payment, the alcalde had paid for them from his personal funds.[42] This case gives us an intimate picture of the paranoia and local strife that resulted from the new obvención laws. We see a clearly distraught cura who suspects enemies everywhere threatening to remove even the last vestige of church income.

We can also see how such desperation caused conflict between the cura and other local officials.

At the same time, even on the eve of the Caste War curas remained important in determining cacique power at the local level. Two cases, one from Dzitbalché and the other from Tixkokob, serve as examples. In October 1840 the cacique of Dzitbalché, Clemente Uc, had to list his assets to prove that he was a man of property in order to justify his right to the post. The problem arose from the fact that the cura was supporting another indígena, Juan Cruz Huchim, as the lawful cacique of Dzitbalché. To overcome the cura's influence, it took not only Uc's testament and proof of solvency but also testimonies of residents and aggressive championing by the teniente of the república de indígenas.[43] In the town of Tixkokob the cura José Clemente Romero took it on himself to oust the cacique Pablo Cauich, who was involved in embezzlement and forcible extraction of taxes from the pueblo residents. The initiative taken by the cura in this case is truly remarkable. He set himself the task of collecting evidence against the cacique. First, he procured testimonies in the form of letters from the important town officials including the alcalde conciliador Justo María Burgos and the juez de paz Francisco Medina. He then forwarded these letters to the governor, which led to the replacement of the cacique on 27 August 1840.[44] Both the cases illustrate that even in the 1840s caciques' power in local society could be affected by the curas.

Thus, in the years leading up to the Caste War interdependence and political alliance remained the order of the day despite the exacerbation of tensions at the local level caused by the new obvención law. However, alliance making was not the only the outcome of cacique interaction with government and church officials. The case of Mauricio May, discussed in chapter 2, whose journeys to Mérida between 1839 and 1841 challenged the power of local officials in Xocén, shows that by 1840 allegiance to the community already held the possibility of an alternative mode of politicization.

In 1833, when the fifty-five-year-old cacique of Tepich, Bautista Canul, fell sick, he could not have anticipated that very shortly he would be incarcerated. He had been summoned by his alcalde to fulfill his duties, which included participating in the cleaning of the streets and plaza of his town, but his health had prevented him from answering the summons. Still, once he felt a little better, Canul went to the cleaning of the cemetery. But by then he had raised the ire of the alcalde José Loreto Vázquez, who saw the cacique's actions as yet another example of his insubordination. It did not help that Canul had already been suspended once from his post.

On 14 July 1833, José Loreto complained of the cacique to his superior, the alcalde conciliador of Tepich.[45] The allegations included not just the cacique's failure to do his duties but also, more ominous, his involvement in inciting indigenous people against paying their taxes. Not long after José Loreto had filed his complaints, Bautista Canul was taken into custody and indígenas of the town began to be summoned for interviews to shed light on the case. As interpreters began questioning the indígenas, interesting new facts surfaced. One indígena, Eusebio Cocom, testified that the cacique had collected money from the villagers in order to obtain an exemption from taxes, especially the obvención, from the government. Eusebio himself had paid ten reales for this purpose. More indígenas were found to be involved. Luciano Cob had paid fourteen reales to the cacique and Laureano Tun had contributed ten reales. Others too had contributed with honey, corn, and chickens. These testimonies point to the fact that by the 1830s taxes weighed so heavily on indigenous communities that indígenas were willing even to pay their cacique if he could help exempt them from taxation, however little chance in reality such a scheme had for success.

Bautista Canul had cleaned cemeteries to be on the good side of the alcalde. He would probably have been surprised to learn that his act of trying to exempt his community from taxes would one day be vindicated by the actions of another cacique of Tepich, Cecilio Chí. The latter, whose name became synonymous with the Caste War of Yucatán, would raise his battle cry in that very same town. Indeed, the origins of the war would lie in this town where in 1847 rumors of a Maya conspiracy in Tepich and the neighboring town of Tihosuco would be the spark that set off one of the longest rebellions in Latin American history. The long struggle over taxation would thus find its ultimate expression.

CHAPTER 4

War and the Cacique

Alliance Making in Caste War Yucatán

The war presented by the Spaniards against the Indians originated in a breach of faith committed by the citizen Don Santiago Imán. In the year thirty-nine, he declared war against the Superior Government of Mexico, alleging as a reason for doing so that it was with a view of liberating the Indians from the payment of contributions. After this war was won by the Indians, the same citizen continued to levy contributions as usual, thus proving himself not to be a man of honor, having forfeited his word with the natives. But the hour has arrived when Christ and his divine mother have given courage to make war against the whites, as we had no money to pay such exactions as the Government thought proper to decree.

God and Liberty,
Cecilio Chí, General
Tepich, 23 April 1849

The coming of the Caste War changed many fortunes in Yucatán; one of these was Andrés Canché's. The war created a new need for caciques. The stability of towns, especially in the face of rebel Maya advances, depended on the loyalty of indigenous communities to the government. It was more necessary than ever to have in place loyal caciques who could provide the necessary glue between indigenous communities and the state. Thus on 2 January 1850, Governor Miguel Barbachano

Parts of this chapter were published in Rajeshwari Dutt, "Crossing Over: Caciques, Indigenous Politics and the Vecino World in Caste War Yucatán," *Ethnohistory* 61, no. 4 (2014): 739–59. Reprinted here with permission of Duke University Press.

issued a decree notifying government officials in the various towns and villages to elect suitable caciques.[1] Accordingly authorities in each pueblo began the task of forwarding names of potential caciques to the government. In the short run, this new bent of policy proved to be beneficial to Canché. On 13 November 1852, the jefe político of Espita recommended the name of Canché as cacique of Cenotillo after consultation with the parish priest.[2]

What was life like for caciques during the region's Caste War, arguably the largest peasant uprising in nineteenth-century Latin American history?[3] When we think of the Caste War, the images of caciques that come to mind are those of warrior-like figures such as Jacinto Pat and Cecilio Chí. But what about nonrebel caciques during this period?[4] Caciques such as Andrés Canché continued to be dependent on the goodwill of local government officials. Yet the war also opened new forms of alliances for nonrebel Maya caciques—alliances through which they were able to protect the interests of their indigenous communities without resorting to rebellion or bloodshed.

CACIQUES DURING THE CASTE WAR

Although innumerable categories of race had been created in the colonial *sistema de castas*, in post-independence Yucatán, for all intents and purposes, there were just two racial and social categories: the Indian and the vecino.[5] The term "vecino" carried connotations of Spanishness, but in practical terms the boundary between the two categories was not always sharp; in documents from the nineteenth century, we occasionally find indigenous people referring to themselves as vecinos (using the term in its connotations of domicile and citizenship).[6] Nevertheless, as long as the repúblicas de indios continued legally to separate indigenous from nonindigenous, society in Yucatán would remain—however problematically—divided into Maya and vecino worlds. The division between the two "races" became most prominent in the minds of Yucatecos and in official rhetoric after the outbreak of violence in 1847.

One of the immediate causes of the Caste War was the revolt by Santiago Imán in 1841. Imán's revolt created, as one scholar describes it, a "welter of expectations" among indigenous Maya, especially around the issue of tax relief. Certainly, other factors played a part, including the steady alienation of indigenous lands, which accelerated in the 1840s. Led by caciques Pat and Chí, indigenous rebels of eastern Yucatán began a veritable war against Yucatecan authorities in July and November 1847. From this point on, the violent confrontation between rebels and government authorities intensified, and the period 1847–52 became the high point of the insurrection.[7]

Government officials consistently portrayed the uprising as a "*guerra de castas*" (caste war) in which indigenous rebel protagonists were waging a violent confrontation against the vecinos. Indigenous people were stereotyped as "barbaric" and "uncivilized." In the backdrop of fear and paranoia among the liberal elite, authorities were now less reticent about reintroducing special laws for indigenous people.[8] In the context of a growing hacienda economy and a lack of sufficient labor, the government now took advantage of the insurrection to institute laws that attempted to force the submission of indigenous laborers to the demands of the new economy. The decree of 27 August 1847 mandated that "vagrancy and idleness will not be permitted among indígenas." To achieve the liberal state objectives, corporal punishment would become an accepted way to force "docility" and "submissiveness" on indigenous people.[9]

The emergence of the Caste War led to the hardening of divisions between the indigenous and vecino worlds in another way too. Though indigenous repúblicas had been officially reinstated in 1824, the first decades after independence saw the progressive proscription of powers previously enjoyed by the repúblicas and their caciques. Significantly, the Constitution of 1841 omitted any mention of indigenous repúblicas and focused instead on elaborating rights and citizenship. All residents of Yucatán who were twenty-one years or above (or eighteen if they were married) were declared citizens.[10] Through this act of omission, the liberal writers of the constitution signaled their ultimate goal: to eliminate corporate privileges of indigenous communities. This denial did not, however, influence reality on the ground, where both repúblicas and their caciques did business as usual. But with the outbreak of war these repúblicas suddenly became important again, as the government sought to retain communities loyal to it and to control the indigenous population. The government saw the Caste War as an expression of the failure of indigenous people to become citizens. Accordingly, the law of 27 August 1847 declared that indigenous people did not have the necessary "aptitude" to enjoy the rights given them in the 1841 constitution and formally restored the separate república system.[11] With this new law, indigenous people were reduced to "tutelage" and denied the automatic rights to citizenship that vecinos enjoyed. It is not hard to see that the liberal government reintroduced the separate indigenous repúblicas (although they had in fact never been abolished) as a punishment to the indigenous people for their role in the Caste War.[12]

Whereas indigenous people were excluded from the universal citizenship that had formed the core of the 1841 constitution, local government officials, in particular the juez de paz, became especially powerful in the years after the outbreak of hostilities. Indeed, as the historian Arturo Güémez Pineda shows, the Caste War period saw an exponential rise in the power of the jueces de paz in Yucatán at the expense of indigenous Maya and their caciques.[13] After the decree of 1847 reemphasized indigenous repúblicas, the government reinstated the juez de paz, an office that had come into being during the centralist years of 1829–31 and 1835–41. With elections to all municipal offices temporarily halted, the juez became a powerful local figure answerable only to the jefe político, the administrative head of the partido.[14] Not only was the juez authorized to administer all local justice, the government made sure that only vecinos could serve in that capacity. The decree of 14 January 1848 declared that only if there was an absolute lack of vecinos could an indigenous person who met all the criteria for the post (wealth, literacy, etc.) fulfill the office of juez.[15] These decrees served to establish the juez as a powerful local official while excluding indigenous people from participating in local governance.

Although low-intensity warfare continued well into the 1860s and even up to the early 1900s, the mid-1850s onward saw a marked reduction in Caste War violence, at least in the nonfrontier areas of Yucatán. Nelson Reed helps us understand this major shift. For the government, he explains, 1855 marked the official end of the Caste War: "There had been no final victory, and there would be fighting for the rest of

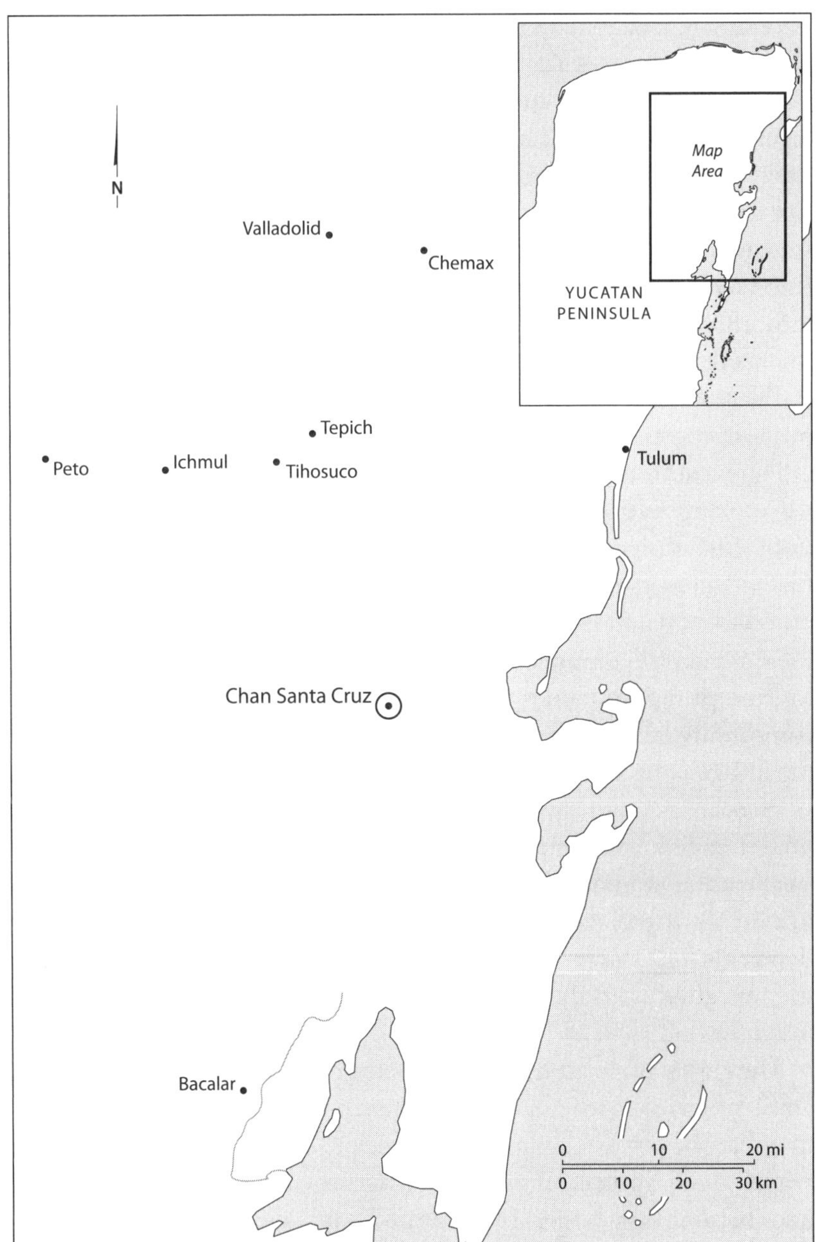

The Caste War shifts to Chan Santa Cruz. Map by Bill Nelson. Copyright © 2017, University of Oklahoma Press.

the century. But after 1855 it was considered a new thing, not a rebellion or a war but a struggle between sovereign powers, Mexico and Chan Santa Cruz."[16] Whether one agrees with Reed or not that 1855 brought an end to the Caste War, what is less ambiguous is that after 1855 Maya rebels retreated southward and the locus of the war shifted to Chan Santa Cruz, a de facto independent state from 1850 to 1893, south of the Yucatán peninsula in what is now the state of Quintana Roo. With the exception of Chan Santa Cruz, in general terms the mid-1850s onward saw peace in the rest of Yucatán, especially in the northwest.

Even though the rebellion had in many ways simmered down in much of the Yucatán, in the late 1850s its effects were still palpable in villages and towns. In 1860 the jefe político of Valladolid described the partido as destroyed and wiped out (*"destruido y aniquilado"*), with the value of property being virtually undermined.[17] In some towns the exigencies of war and demands of the government combined to threaten the subsistence of the indígenas there. In 1862 the cacique and the república of Tixkokob pleaded with the government to exempt the indígenas of the town from the *fagina* labor (unpaid community labor such as public works).[18] The cacique explained that the indígenas of the town had happily served the needs of the *división de operaciones* (military operations division) when they had been stationed in Tixkokob. In fact, a segment of the population continued to serve in this role. Yet the inhabitants of the town were still expected to provide their labor in public works such as road building. These demands left nearly no time for cultivating their fields. The cacique thus pleaded with the government to exempt his town from fagina labor for one year.

The Caste War had mixed results for caciques. Rugeley shows the ambiguous role of caciques during this period, in which they were as likely to suppress rebellion as to support it. As the most visible and arguably most powerful indigenous figures in their communities, caciques became easy targets of government ire. In certain cases, as in that of the cacique of Motul, Bacelino May, suspicion led to arrest and then finally summary execution.[19] At the same time, the very influence caciques exercised in their communities made the government see them as valuable allies. For the government, alliance with a cacique was important because the cacique could use his local influence to keep his particular community loyal. At times the government sought to cement alliance with a cacique by offering him the title of *hidalgo.* Apart from a social leg up, the hidalgo status came with practical perks and often involved tax forgiveness and other benefits. In January 1848, for instance, the cacique of Saban, Felipe Cauich, was rewarded with the title of hidalgo and exemption from paying the *contribución personal* (personal tax) for life.[20] To secure an alliance with the cacique Jacinto Pat, Governor Barbachano sent him a shoulder band with words "*Gran Cacique de Yucatán*" inscribed in gold letters.[21] Thus, the Caste War proved to be a double-edged sword for caciques. The caciques' balancing act—of simultaneously representing the community and acting as brokers for the government—had become more difficult than ever, but allying with the government held the possibility of greater power, privileges, and acceptance into vecino society.

Nevertheless, Caste War violence had severe effects even on loyal caciques. Though military hidalgo status promised higher standing to some caciques who fought on the government side, many other loyal caciques suffered the consequences of the war. Such was the case for Bernardino Tzakum, the cacique of Yaxcabá for eight years, who by 1857 had reached the point of despair and filed a *renuncia* (resignation) to leave his position.[22] According to Tzakum's testimony, the invading rebels had reduced his pueblo to a condition of misery. The losses suffered by Tzakum together with his old age and infirmities were cited as the reasons for his renuncia. Tzakum's case shows that a long tenure as a cacique was no guarantee of a prosperous life, especially during the Caste War. Tzakum was only one of many caciques who became progressively more impoverished by the 1860s. Nicolás Uh, who had served five years as cacique in the town of Oxkutzcab, also tendered his resignation, in 1856, the main reason being poverty and that he could no longer support himself.[23]

Although being recognized as a military hidalgo brought some reprieve from taxes and contributions, monetarily the post of cacique brought no real reward. Caciques still depended for their subsistence on cultivating their own milpas. In many cases, because of old age, illness, or poverty a cacique could no longer cultivate his lands or pay another person to do so for him. Renuncias by caciques have this common theme of destitution. It is possible that such caciques were not all genuinely ill; some may have used ill health as an excuse to leave their positions. However, even if that were the case, these renuncias suggest that the post was no longer lucrative or desirable.

Renouncing a cacique post did not guarantee being relieved from the post. Renuncias had to be approved by government authorities, and in some cases the slim pool of "qualified" indígenas in the pueblo meant that an ex-cacique could be summoned back to office. This was the case for Manuel Couoh, cacique of Izamal. In 1857, Couoh renounced his post after serving for six years.[24] Like many other caciques of the period, he cited ill health as the main reason for resignation. The government at the time accepted the renuncia. However, five years later Manuel Couoh again emerges in the documents. We learn that the cacique of Izamal in 1862, Juan de Dios Mut, had resigned his post and Manuel Couoh was brought back to serve.[25]

Throughout the late 1850s and early 1860s, the role of government in indigenous life continued very much as it had before. If anything, the government tried to exert even more authority over indigenous communities in a bid to prevent indígenas from joining rebels or undermining the government war on rebels. In some cases, cacique privileges were even more threatened. In the suburb of Santa Ana in 1856, for instance, the cacique's role as tax collector came under attack. In correspondence to the jefe político of Mérida, the subdelegado Pedro Rubio wrote that the cacique was not able to guarantee collection of taxes from indígenas.[26] According to Rubio, the cacique was continually drunk and lacked the wealth to compensate any failures. To remedy this situation, the subdelegados of Mérida installed vecinos to collect taxes in place of the cacique. This action on the part of subdelegados signaled an intervention into a role that had been fulfilled by caciques since independence. As well as inserting a vecino into indígena life, this surely undermined the cacique's authority in the town.

Other subtle changes can also be noticed in this period, such as with the selection of caciques. Throughout the colonial and early national periods, the ritual of naming ternas had signified a pact between the indigenous república and the government (see chapter 1). But official documents show a subtle change in this regard in the late 1850s and early 1860s. In Ticul in 1861, for instance, a cacique resigned and another was named in his place.[27] No list or terna was mentioned. Rather the document simply named the cacique who would be replacing the outgoing cacique. If, as the document suggests, the terna was not held, then this implies a change in the way the indigenous repúblicas and the government interacted. Since this ritual had always symbolically reiterated the importance of indigenous repúblicas in naming their own leader, its absence in this case shows that the importance of indigenous repúblicas had started to wane, especially in the eyes of the government.

In other ways, the relationship between government and indigenous communities continued much as before. His relations with local government officials still remained tantamount to preserving a cacique's power. Thus we see collusion between jueces de paz and caciques, as in the case of the cacique José María Pech, who together with the juez de paz Eusebio Gallegos was accused of abuse of authority in the town of Suma in 1862.[28] Caciques still interacted with the government on a day-to-day basis through their relations with local officials and could be ousted from their position by these officials if they failed to maintain a cooperative relationship with them.

In general, then, the effects of the Caste War years on caciques were contradictory. They brought misery to many a cacique, whether in the form of illness or loss of property; but they also helped to slow the process of liberal reform that aimed to do away with the repúblicas and cacique privileges. The status of the cacique had begun a steady decline from the moment of independence in 1821. By the 1830s and '40s the only official role left to the cacique was that of collecting taxes and surveillance of indigenous populations to prevent dispersal, or "vagrancy"—essentially because the government realized that the cacique would be more successful in doing this than any vecino. Indeed, the post of cacique had even been abolished by the liberal state following independence, only to be brought back in 1824 because of these practical exigencies. Even then, the government remained committed to reducing the power of indigenous repúblicas. It is likely that, had the Caste War not erupted, this goal would have taken its logical course and the repúblicas as well as the caciques would have been abolished permanently.

Instead, with the advent of the rebellion loyalty of indigenous communities became paramount for the government. Caciques, who as leaders of these communities exercised influence and de facto power over them, thus became important allies of the government. It is true that the government's need for loyal caciques in some ways made them more vulnerable. Caciques suspected of collusion with the rebels became victims of a veritable witch hunt. This was true even in the early 1860s. In 1861, the jefe político of Mérida proposed replacing the cacique of Yzimná simply because some town vecinos alleged that he was untrustworthy.[29] Yet it is also true that caciques who remained loyal to the government were for the first time in a long time given a certain security. They were in effect given much higher social standing than before. Many caciques were provided incentives such as hidalgo status, especially if they participated in military expeditions against rebel enemies. The importance of caciques, which had been waning since the 1820s, thus saw resurgence in some ways during the Caste War period. In an ironic way, although the rebellion weakened indigenous communities, it also helped to ensure the survival of the indigenous repúblicas and loyal caciques into the 1860s.

CACIQUES AND THEIR JUECES: THE CASE OF ANGELINO UICAB

On 7 April 1851 the cacique of Teya, Angelino Uicab, presented a petition to the governor in Mérida.[30] Uicab complained that the juez de paz of Teya, José Lugardo Barcelón, abused the indigenous people by demanding excessive fagina labor and was now trying to use Uicab himself to achieve his objectives; the juez was making him recruit workers and also was using him as a middleman to negotiate work between the juez and the Maya. With this arrangement, if the indigenous workers complained, the blame would fall on the cacique's door because "they had been obligated to work by his [Uicab's] hands." Uicab refused to be a part of this charade and appealed to the governor to resolve this situation.

Though not in the epicenter of hostilities, Teya nevertheless was not untouched by the violence of the Caste War. In 1848, for instance, both the town of Teya and the auxiliary town of Tepakam were occupied and set on fire by rebels.[31] An absence of similar reports from 1850–51 suggests that rebel activity in the Teya region had been contained, but the government continued to station troops in cantons around the town, suggesting that fear of rebellion remained. Angelino Uicab's petition seems to have resonated with Governor Barbachano, who responded almost immediately in a brief note sent to the jefe político of Motul, Andrés de Zepeda. The governor instructed that under no pretext should jueces use caciques to force indígenas to work in the fields. Rather, Barbachano recommended that the laborers be contracted directly and should themselves reach an agreement with whoever was hiring them to decide the right price for their labor. By the beginning of 1851, news of the apparition of the miraculous "speaking cross" (which "spoke" to the indígenas and assured them of victory) had spread through the peninsula and galvanized a group of rebels.[32] Faced with the prospect of losing a loyal indigenous community during a time of rebellion, the governor solidly took the side of the cacique against the juez. This response perhaps also shows that the cacique was still important. He was seen as a vital ally of the government, especially in maintaining peace and order during a time of chaos and upheaval. To ensure that this relationship remained intact, the government was willing to threaten harsh consequences on its own officials and functionaries.

The juez de paz José Lugardo Barcelón and vecino residents of Teya in his circle seem to have gotten wind of the fact that Angelino Uicab had left the pueblo to go to Mérida to complain to the governor. In early April 1851, Barcelón drew up a letter to the governor signed by himself, the parish cura, and five other vecinos including José Gregorio Lara and Francisco Leal. From other documents pertaining to Teya we know that Leal was Barcelón's *primero funcionario* (first officer). Although none of the documents pertaining to the 1851 Teya case makes this explicit, it appears that Don Gregorio Lara was the *juez segundo* of Teya—the juez de paz immediately below the rank of Barcelón.[33] In the letter to the governor the jueces and others complained against Angelino Uicab. They claimed that shortly after his elevation to the rank of hidalgo the cacique had openly started defending and protecting *"a su raza indígena,"* his "Indian" race. Uicab had set himself up as a "sultan" in the pueblo, they claimed. He frequently held loud *reuniones* (meetings) in his house—sites of drunkenness and debauchery, with the cacique's drinking continuing for hours after the meetings. Several times he had been found unconscious in a drunken stupor on the side of the street after a night of revelry. Barcelón and the other signatories to this letter denounced the cacique as scandalous, loud, and, most important, *"declarado enemigo de nuestra raza"*—a declared enemy of our (i.e., white) race.

Lugardo Barcelón and his associates' letter to the governor was a full-fledged denouncement. Barcelón and his cosignatories portrayed Uicab as a traitor on several levels. Because he was a newly minted hidalgo, Uicab's attempt to subvert indigenous commoners by denouncing the local authorities could be construed as nothing short of total betrayal of trust. That he was holding loud reuniones in his house only served to bolster the accusations of betrayal and subversion. The government had always seen holding loud and tumultuous meetings as a sign of subversion and a threat to village social order. Working through archival documents in the decades after independence, we can find repeated cases of caciques being reprimanded or worse for holding such meetings. In Tekax in 1845, for instance, the cacique of Peto, Macedonio Dzul, came under criticism and a case was filed against him for holding a *"reunion tumultuaria y asonada"*—a loud and disorderly meeting.[34] Similarly, in 1842 the cacique of Yaxkukul was arrested by the alcalde of the pueblo for "loud and disorderly behavior."[35] During the Caste War, wealthy vecino residents of pueblos lived in constant fear that indígenas of their pueblos would join the rebels. As the war gained momentum, the government was always afraid that the loyal pueblos would be subverted and take the side of the rebel indígenas. Their fears were not unfounded. In 1847, for instance, a letter from rebel leaders Chí and Pat to the cacique of Kancabdzonot, Francisco Camal, inviting the latter to join arms with the rebels had been intercepted by the government.[36] Nor could the government ever forget that these two main rebel leaders were themselves caciques. Though rowdy behavior seems to have been cause for reprimands in the years before the Caste War, this same conduct in the context of rebellion and upheaval could be seen as a veritable threat to the social order.

April 1851 witnessed further verbal attacks on Angelino Uicab. On 15 April, Don Barcelón and the *comandante militar* (military commander), Buenaventura Criollo, wrote to the jefe político in Motul, Andrés De Zepeda, about the misconduct of Uicab. Barcelón and Criollo were writing as representatives of the Sociedad Patriótica de Motul (Patriotic Society of Motul). Patriotic societies seem to have been in operation both before and after independence in 1821. Some had formed during the turbulent years of Yucatán's wars with Mexico. They served broad economic and political functions.[37] The Sociedad Patriótica of Motul had the economic function in this particular case of raising food for the soldiers and their families stationed in the military cantons around Motul. Even though Motul was relatively well off, Yucatán as a whole was experiencing severe grain shortages in the 1850s.[38] As early as August 1848, we find correspondence between the jefe político Andrés de Zepeda and the governor in which the former expressed his worries about the difficulties of collecting grain to send to soldiers and their families.[39]

In their letter, Barcelón and Criollo stated that they had been appointed by the Sociedad Patriótica of Motul to promote donation of grain by the indigenous residents of Teya for troops stationed south and east of the state of Yucatán, focal areas of Caste War hostilities. They complained that Uicab had seized the entire quantity of grain donated, purportedly to send to the *tesorero general* (treasurer) in Mérida. They accused the cacique of openly manifesting "dedication to and protection of his Indian race" and expressed the fear that such behavior could ultimately serve to foster a revolt (*sublevación*).

Barcelón and Criollo's letter was meant to be a damning accusation of the cacique. Using racializing rhetoric, the two men tried to represent the conflict between Uicab and themselves not as about questions of labor but rather as fundamentally racial, with the cacique protecting his "Indian" race. And though their intent was to discredit the cacique, it is possible that Barcelón and Criollo were presenting what they thought was the truth about the cacique's behavior. Whatever the case may have been, the ultimate effect of the letter was to portray the cacique as unpatriotic, disorderly, and even subversive. In this the two men were also feeding into the official rhetoric, which characterized the Caste War primarily as a race war.

Upon receiving the missive from Barcelón and Criollo representing the Sociedad Patriótica, Andrés de Zepeda sprang into action. In a communication drawn up on 19 April 1851, Zepeda sought the help of the juez de paz of the neighboring town of Cansahcab, Don Buenaventura Castillo (not to be confused with comandante militar, Buenaventura Criollo) to resolve the situation in Teya. Zepeda gathered the documents pertaining to the case and sent this bundle of papers to the juez of Cansahcab.

Buenaventura Castillo undertook the task of investigating the truth behind the allegations made by the various parties involved in the Teya case, including the vecinos, the juez, the indígenas, and the cacique. On 26 April 1851, Castillo sent his report to Andrés de Zepeda. The interviews that formed part of the report offer us important insights into the case. Castillo interviewed several key individuals including Uicab and his teniente, Benancio Ek. The latter in his testimony explained that the cacique had held a reunion in his house with the purpose of raising money to appeal to the governor and request the removal of the jueces and their replacement with other individuals whom they wanted. According to Ek, the cacique asked certain indígenas of the community to contribute two reales and others a chicken each. Those testifying differed in their accounts of what was done with the money thus raised. Some suggested that the contributions raised were sent to the *secretario de gobierno* (secretary of the government) in Mérida.

In response to reports coming from Teya, the secretario general in Mérida, Francisco Martínez de Arredondo, appealed to the juez de primera instancia of Izamal to investigate the case. In his letter dated 19 May 1851, Arredondo stressed that the honor of the office of the secretaria was at stake and hence the juez must find out what happened to the money and the grain that had supposedly been given to that office. Arredondo also wrote that he had found that the chickens had been given to one Enrique Manzanero of the neighborhood of Mérida. To get to the bottom of the allegations, the magistrate in Izamal conducted his own investigations by interviewing some of the key witnesses.

Piecing together the information in the various testimonies, an interesting aspect of the Teya case emerges: the cacique did not just form alliances with other indígenas but also with certain vecinos. The teniente Benancio Ek's testimony pointed to the fact that Uicab raised money for his trip to Mérida to meet the governor in two ways. He raised contributions in the form of money and chickens, but also, significantly, he *"vendido al trabajo"* ("sold to work," i.e., made to work to generate money) indígenas who could not contribute in either form to Don Gregorio Lara, the juez segundo, that is, the official second to Lugardo Barcelón in importance in Teya. A second nonindigenous person who allied with the cacique was one Don Enrique Manzanero.

In his testimony, Uicab stated that he had collected a total of fourteen pesos and sixty chickens from the indígenas of his pueblo. This included nine pesos, which was the cost incurred by the indígenas to make the petitions. The balance of five pesos and sixty chickens was gifted to Enrique Manzanero, *"quien nos prestaba todos estos servicios"* ("who did all these services for us"). We can only guess at what these "services" were. But it seems likely that Manzanero, a vecino from Mérida, presented himself to the cacique and the other indígenas as a government insider. He reportedly told them that he had worked in the secretario general's office. Thus, he presented himself as knowledgeable about how the government offices worked and as willing to help the cacique present his case before the government. It is quite possible that Manzanero took advantage of the cacique's inexperience with the workings of the government in Mérida and positioned himself as an authority on the matter. In that sense, it seems likely that the cacique's decision to go to the governor and even the way that he planned the presentation was influenced in one way or another by Enrique Manzanero. Although we will probably never know, it is likely that this obscure vecino resident of Mérida played a larger role than many others involved in this case.

The testimonies made in Izamal also shed light on one more mystery surrounding the Teya case: the fate of the grain and beans seized by the cacique from the Sociedad Patriótica. In his account, the cacique confessed that he had assigned three indígenas to take the grain to Mérida and hand it over to Manzanero. According to Angelino Uicab he had sent the grain to Manzanero so that the latter could hand it over to the *tesoreria general* (treasurer). Manzanero had even sent Uicab a receipt showing that he had sent the grain to the treasury as promised. Looking back at the testimonies, one is struck by the cacique's complete confidence in Enrique Manzanero. It is possible that Manzanero had in fact taken advantage of the cacique's trust in him and swindled him by appropriating the grain himself rather than sending it to the treasury as he claimed. Unfortunately for us, the case of Angelino Uicab and indígenas versus juez Lugardo Barcelón ends with these testimonies. On 26 May 1851, the magistrate of Izamal declared that there was "no sufficient merit to continue the proceedings." The arbiters of justice had already reached a definite conclusion. On the same day, Uicab was removed from his post for his misconduct and Benancio Ek, his teniente, was raised to the post of cacique of Teya.[40] We will never know whether the treasury ever received any of the grain, but what we do know about the case provides rare insights into nineteenth-century town politics.

Located in the northwest of Yucatán, Teya had a sizeable nonindigenous population. In 1821 the parish Teya recorded 196 vecinos and 821 indios.[41] Thus, at the start of the early national period vecinos accounted for about a quarter of the total population. One of the unexpected aspects of the case involving Angelino Uicab is the alliance he formed with non-indígenas. One of these was Enrique Manzanero, whose role we have already touched on. However, Manzanero seems to have been a resident of Mérida rather than Teya. To understand how the vecino world of Teya influenced the outcome of the case, we need look no further than Don Gregorio Lara.

Angelino Uicab seems to have forged a major alliance with Don Gregorio Lara, juez segundo of Teya. From independent testimonies collected by both Buenaventura Castillo and the juez in Izamal, we know that Lara fulfilled a crucial role in the cacique's attempt to raise money to finance his trip to the governor in Mérida. When the cacique asked the indígenas in Teya for contributions, those who could not were "*vendidos al trabajo*" to Gregorio Lara. We must ask what prompted Don Gregorio Lara to ally with the cacique. The answer lies in the politics within the white vecino community in Teya at that time and comes through most clearly in two cases recorded after the conclusion of the case of Angelino Uicab, in 1852 and 1853.

About a year after the conclusion of the Uicab case, another case against Lara shook the calm of Teya's vecino community. On 6 August

1852, a vecino resident of Teya, Gregorio Escalante, accused Lara of abusing authority by compromising the honor of Escalante's wife.[42] The juez primero Lugardo Barcelón was one of the first to testify on Escalante's behalf and concurred that Lara had taken the woman from Escalante's house and maintained her in his own. On his part, Lara claimed that everyone in the pueblo would attest to his innocence other than the supporters of Barcelón and his officer, Francisco Leal. Lara explained that Barcelón and Leal resented him because he had decried many of their criminal actions; they never let a chance pass to exercise their vengeance on him. Lara's words seem to suggest that the strained relations between these men had a long history.

In February 1853, Gregorio Lara was acquitted of the charges brought against him by Gregorio Escalante and was let off with a mild rebuke that he needed to conduct himself with more delicacy and circumspection. However, a few months later another scandal enveloped Lara. He was accused of "public concubinage," for living with a woman named Isabel Meña without being married to her.[43] Lara had come to Teya in 1846, accompanied by this same Isabel Meña. He maintained that she was his housekeeper and that they had no illicit relationship. Rather, Lara claimed that Lugardo Barcelón was conspiring to drive him out of Teya. While he had been away in Mérida, Lara asserted, Barcelón's men had gone to his house, dragged out Meña, and publicly displayed her in the plaza in shackles; there were many witnesses, including the entire república de indígenas of Teya. Nevertheless, the case was finally settled against Lara; the government considered removing him from his post in Teya, and he was ordered to remove himself from "public concubinage" with Isabel Meña.[44]

Whether or not justice was done in this case, it provides us valuable insight into the relationship between the two jueces—a relationship of deep and bitter animosity and conflict that dated to well before it was expressed and recorded in 1852 and 1853 cases. The 1853 case suggests that Lara saw himself as a champion of the indigenous inhabitants of Teya and viewed Uicab's own antagonist, Lugardo Barcelón, as scheming and abusive. Even though this case is set almost two years after the Uicab case, understanding this strained relationship between the two jueces can be very valuable in explaining why Gregorio Lara allied with the cacique.

The alliances Uicab formed extended beyond the pale of the indigenous community he represented. Two critical alliances—one with Enrique Manzanero and the other with Gregorio Lara—would be important elements of Uicab's struggle against juez Lugardo Barcelón. These alliances show that race was not always the determining factor in relationships between indigenous and vecinos during the Caste War. This is not to dismiss the importance of race; the events of the Caste War show that race could be and was the operative principle in many instances. However, in this particular case, other factors were primary.

ANDRÉS CANCHÉ IN THE 1850s: CHANGING FORTUNES IN THE EARLY YEARS OF WAR

At about the same time the case of Angelino Uicab was drawing to a close, Andrés Canché's fortunes too were beginning to change. In the center of the war-torn region around Valladolid, Cenotillo had become an important area for the government to retain control over. The first year of hostilities witnessed uncertainty and panic among the vecino population, but by 1848 the Yucatecan war effort under General López de Llergo was beginning to turn the tide against the rebels. The year 1848 witnessed a decisive turnaround in Cenotillo as well. Until this time, Cenotillo seemed to have been a refuge area for rebels from the adjoining towns. In 1848, for instance, Yucatecan troops claimed to have tracked down rebels who had taken refuge in hacienda Tachhebila in Cenotillo.[45] In fact, when the troops finally entered the hacienda they found utensils left behind that suggested that these indígenas were mere vagrants, but the military remained convinced that these interlopers were rebels. The Yucatecan military attacked the town of Cenotillo to drive out what it viewed as rebels amassing there, and by July 1848 government forces had occupied the town.[46] Thus, by the early 1850s Cenotillo appears to have been a government stronghold.

On 22 November 1852, Canché was once more named to the post of cacique of Cenotillo.[47] His return to the post of cacique indicates that he had managed to retain a degree of influence in Cenotillo despite being out of office for years. According to the jefe político, Canché had all the desired qualifications necessary to be the new cacique. Thus, despite losing much of his wealth and property after the embezzlement case of 1837, somehow Canché had managed to reinstate himself as a man of means and status. He was obviously also seen as a loyal indígena, someone who would maintain the stability of the town and protect it from rebel incursion. It is also possible that the memory of Canché's previous transgression had now dimmed in the minds of the authorities, especially in the face of the now much more pressing challenge of securing loyal pueblos amid the Caste War.

Being back in power did not, however, mean the end of Canché's struggle as a local political figure. A new case directed against the cacique would bring into question his suitability to act as the state's chosen representative of Cenotillo's indígenas. On 15 December 1855, the juez de paz of Cenotillo, Felipe Correa, and the parish priest of the town, Jorge Burgos, appealed to the jefe político of Espita, Marcos Peniche, to effect the removal of Canché from his post.[48] With the priest on his side, Correa brought before the jefe político allegations that Canché had become a threat to public order in Cenotillo. Correa alleged that after becoming cacique Canché had become disobedient and insubordinate. He appealed to Peniche to relieve Canché of his post not only for the public good but to preserve tranquility in the town.

With the outbreak of the Caste War, a general sense of paranoia had swept through Yucatán. One effect of this troubled atmosphere was persecution of caciques—even to the point of murder, such as in the village of Tabi in 1847 where the cacique and other members of the indigenous república were assassinated.[49] Canché's previous record of embezzling public funds would have had a corroborative effect on the general picture of misconduct that the juez Correa was trying to paint. Correa observed that the past subprefectura had also been aware of Canché's excesses. Yet, despite the fact that Correa was presenting serious allegations against Canché, he was careful to do so in a way that would prevent unnecessary tumult in Cenotillo. An examination of this aspect of Correa's appeal helps to underline the power and influence that Canché must have held in Cenotillo.

In his appeal to the government Correa emphasized that his purpose was not to complain against Andrés Canché but rather to remedy the ill effects of his tenure by proposing a replacement for him. He seemed to want to show the replacement of Canché as arising naturally rather than by any intervention on his part. The timing of his petition itself is an indication of this. The juez de paz was writing to the government in December 1855. The end of the calendar year had been the customary time when new officers for indigenous repúblicas were chosen and elected so that they could begin in office from the start of the next year. Correa makes this intention explicit when he writes, "As the renewal of the republicas de indígenas of this town is approaching . . . we are making a formal request for his removal through a smooth political means and not scandalous."[50] Clearly, Correa was being cautious—cautious not to raise any kind of scandal in Cenotillo, and cautious not to appear to be the cause of Canché's dismissal. That Correa was afraid that an outright removal of Canché would cause tumult in Cenotillo is indicative of Canché's standing in his community. His own desire to distance himself from the removal shows that Correa felt apprehensive about a possible backlash by the community against himself. So, although Correa's appeal was not meant to voice the desires of the community, in the end it did so effectively, showing the extent of Canché's power and the community's support for him.

Interestingly, Correa's proposed replacement for Canché was none other than Canché's longtime associate, escribano Feliciano Couoh. In proposing the name of Couoh, Correa was not departing much from established practice. Indeed throughout the nineteenth century escribanos used literacy to ascend the social ladder and become caciques themselves. For instance, German Che, cacique of Espita, had served ten years as escribano to his predecessor before himself becoming cacique.[51] Similarly, Anselmo Kenel, cacique of Xul, had served as escribano to the community for thirteen years before becoming cacique in January 1842.[52] Ten years later, when the death of Nunkini cacique Apolonio Trejo necessitated an election, Francisco Ek, the escribano of the community, was chosen.[53] And it was the literacy and education gained during his four-year stint as escribano that recommended Luciano Mis as the cacique of Dzitbalché in 1837.[54]

In a way, escribanos were best positioned to take over the role of caciques in their pueblos. They had been the right-hand men of the caciques. Escribanos accompanied the cacique in many tasks such as going around to collect taxes. Caciques who were illiterate in Spanish relied on escribanos to write reports and to sign official documents on their behalf. Indeed, throughout colonial times and even after independence, the one person in the community to be literate had been the escribano. For repúblicas themselves, it is certainly not hard to see that it was much better for the community to recommend the name of an escribano to the post of cacique in the instance of the death of the cacique or renunciation of the post, since there would be some continuity in terms of the relationship between the community and the república. In naming Feliciano Couoh, juez de paz Correa was also ensuring that the new cacique would gain acceptance in his community, thus preventing any scandal or instability that Canché's departure might cause. The juez also pointed out that, apart from being intelligent and capable, Feliciano Couoh was also docile (*dócil*)—a contrast to Canché's "natural insubordination." In a time of uncertainty and war, Couoh seemed to be the perfect replacement for Canché, and his past involvement in the embezzlement case was conveniently forgotten.

ANDRÉS CANCHÉ IN THE 1860s: THE STRUGGLE FOR COMMUNITY LAND

Land usage became a central issue in the Caste War, and an issue that would return Andrés Canché to the scene in 1863. The peculiarities of Maya cultivation practices had important repercussions during the years leading up to the war. Maya farmers practiced slash-and-burn, or swidden, agriculture. A considerable amount of land had to lie fallow for a specified period to absorb the nutrients in the ash after being cleared and burned. Often the Maya left the boundaries of their *ejido* (common land) in search of cultivable land elsewhere. This sort of shifting cultivation had characterized Maya agriculture since pre-Columbian times and became a problem only with the colonial state imposing territorial boundaries demarcating lands of one pueblo from another. Even then the colonial policy of keeping Maya tied to particular pieces of land through mechanisms such as reducciones proved to be a failure. The Maya ability to maintain their way of cultivation would, however, be irrevocably threatened in the 1840s.

One of the main reasons for the Caste War, according to the historian Terry Rugeley, was the progressive alienation of land experienced by the peasantry in Yucatán. After Imán's revolt and the return of federalism in Yucatán, the state established a series of reforms that presaged the later tenets of La Reforma, a period of intense liberal land reforms under Benito Juárez throughout Mexico. Beginning one of the biggest land grabs in Mexican history, the Yucatecan government passed legislation on 5 April 1841 limiting the size of community ejidos to one square league around the village church.[55] As Rugeley notes, "In one stroke, the liberals eliminated whatever legal basis the peasant farmers might claim for maintaining milpa outside a limited confine." Given the shifting cultivation practiced by Maya farmers, this legislation was a significant source of disquiet among the rural peasantry. Article 4 of the 5 April decree also indicated areas of land that could be sold or transferred, but at that time these were mostly lands in the frontier areas such as Bacalar and Seibaplaya. In November 1843, however, the alienation of land became a serious problem. On 16 November the government issued a decree that opened the way for land to be parceled out as compensation for participation in the recent military campaigns.[56] Not only soldiers, but those who had loaned money to the government such as landowners, entrepreneurs, and priests became beneficiaries of this new decree. In all, almost 460,000 hectares of land were alienated as a result of these decrees. Since most of this was fallow land that had been cleared and burned as an integral part of Maya swidden cultivation, these rulings altered a traditional peasant way of life that had been maintained for generations.[57]

The years after the outbreak of the Caste War progressively worsened the situation for Maya peasants. The decrees of the 1840s had fattened the purses of certain landowners and led to the growth of haciendas, but the rebellion wrought havoc upon the hacendado class. Maya rebels who had taken up arms to resist land alienation saw haciendas as emblematic of the economic developments that had disempowered them. Scores of haciendas were attacked and left in ruin. According to census data, in the districts of Valladolid and Tekax, for instance, 52 percent of haciendas were destroyed between 1845 and

1862.[58] Those haciendas that were spared suffered from a lack of farmhands. As the Maya peasantry joined rebel groups, or alternately became targets of these rebels for not joining their cause, the number of *acasillados*, those who would labor on haciendas, became less and less. The lack of indígenas to tend the grazing lands of the montes meant a lack of pasture for livestock. Thus, the war affected both types of haciendas—those that cultivated crops like sugar and those that engaged in livestock farming.

After the initial years of hardship, and as the Yucatecan state began to push the rebels to the southern edges of the state, hacendados attempted to recoup their losses, and the atmosphere of racial hatred generated by the rebellion aided them. In this "hardening regime of class and racial domination," hacendados and other vecino landowners could now "brush aside whatever impediments the republics and their caciques still presented." The wider vecino fear of indígenas who had wreaked such havoc meant that actions that previously would have never have been socially accepted now became the order of the day: "Municipal officials carved up areas of the común to facilitate their sale to family and friends. Landowners who earlier had occupied lands for open cattle ranches now enclosed them, converting them into haciendas. They erected stone landmarks in woodlands adjacent to their properties and hired surveyors to the lands and map them, now without need for the consent of indigenous officials."[59] With local government officials such as jueces de paz themselves being landowners who participated in displacing indígenas, government efforts proved impotent in protecting indigenous people from the hacendados.[60] Indeed, by 1860 the government had begun to pass laws that actually accelerated the process of dispossession of indigenous people from their lands.

The Caste War also brought significant changes to one of the predominant types of haciendas in mid-nineteenth-century Yucatán—cattle ranches. Before the war, the government had always sought to protect land from incursion by cattle because of the inevitable destruction that came with unregulated grazing. Even as late as 1844, the government passed laws designed to protect land from cattle incursion. The decree of 23 November 1844 prohibited the establishment of new cattle populations without express license from the government and dictated that cattle could not be grazed within one league of a hacienda.[61] But in the wake of the war's destruction and the growing economic burdens of the state, the government changed its tune. In its decree of 3 July 1860, the government instituted special laws for the duration of the Caste War with regards to livestock raising. Explaining that the prolongation of the war had led to the disappearance of livestock farming along the line of defense, causing the economy of these areas to suffer greatly, the government sought to remedy the situation by instituting new special protective measures to encourage the breeding of livestock. According to the decree, owners of livestock now had permission to graze cattle in areas of pueblos in the districts of Valladolid, Espita, Tizimín, Peto, and Tekax. Residents of these areas would have to fence in their cultivable land to protect it from the cattle, since the government would not be liable for any damages.[62] One can imagine the impunity with which owners of livestock haciendas now took advantage of these new policies.[63]

The decree of 3 July 1860 also brought the return of Andrés Canché, whom we last saw in 1855 facing allegations of insubordination, to the archival records. We find a joint petition from October 1863 addressed from Canché and the commander of the national guard, Don Buenaventura Cabrera, to the governor of Yucatán protesting the implementation of the 3 July decree in Cenotillo.[64] The petition reveals that Canché is at this time the cacique of Cenotillo. Whether this means that he had not been removed in 1855 or had returned to power is unclear, since there are no relevant extant documents for the interim years. In any case, when Canché reemerges in the documents in 1863, he does so not as the lone embattled cacique of the past but as one with powerful friends.

The alliance between Buenaventura Cabrera and Andrés Canché—one a military commander fighting Maya rebels, the other an indigenous cacique with a record of insubordination—may appear unlikely at first glance. But their joint petition reveals the deeper issues that brought these two together. In it, Cabrera was representing the interests of the *subordinados* (subordinates) in the army and other affected vecinos, and the cacique was representing the interests of the indigenous community. The two asserted that as a result of the new law the entire pueblo was suffering ("*sufre este pueblo sus grabes y fatales consecuencias*"). The law had allowed any landowner to use whatever land he wanted to raise livestock. Cabrera and Canché declared that the people of Cenotillo had been entangled in the war without any kind of help in sight. Now the decree had made things worse. There was a shortage of grain, and with livestock infiltrating the land many vecinos and indígenas would be reduced to slavery or would have to emigrate.

Cabrera and Canché found common cause because each was responsible for a part of the community of Cenotillo that was victim of this new decree. Canché, as a cacique, sought to protect the indígenas whose milpas had been beset by the invading cattle. Cabrera owed his allegiance to his soldiers stationed in Cenotillo, for whom the crops grown nearby were the only form of sustenance in the absence of rations and supplies from an already financially extended state. Thus the two petitioners declared that the only hope for the poor soldiers and indígenas was their milpas. Canché and Cabrera explained that in the past the owners of livestock had had to ask for permission from the government to establish *crías de ganado* (livestock raising). Now, with the decree, the "*señores del ganado*" simply took whatever land they wanted, which included the best land of the ejido. These livestock owners were also accustomed to burning thousands of acres of the ejido annually to clear the land for their livestock, which day by day reduced the montes. The petition also reminded the governor of the strategic nature of Cenotillo as the "*unicamente punto que integra el partido de Espita*" ("unique point that integrates the district of Espita") and its importance as a bastion of government power in the war against the *bárbaros*. The petitioners acknowledged that in 1860, when the law was put into force, there had indeed been a shortage of livestock in the region, but three years on that was no longer the case. They ended with the request that livestock owners be asked to move their cattle to a different location.

The alliance between Canché and Cabrera thus arose out of a shared concern for the residents of Cenotillo in the context of the Caste War. Had there not been an ongoing war in which the stability of pueblos and especially the loyalty of the indigenous residents were so important, it is likely that such an alliance would never have taken place.

For a brief moment, though, poor residents of Cenotillo—whether vecino or indigenous—were united in common cause against the cattle ranchers. And in this contest, their chosen champions were a military commander and an extremely familiar face in Cenotillo, Andrés Canché.

Canché and Cabrera's petition proved successful. On 15 October 1863, the governor, Felipe Navarette, acceded to the request on the grounds that the residents of the pueblo of Cenotillo were patriotic and had always done their service *"a la causa de the civilización que sostiene el Estado contra los indios sublevados"* ("for the cause of civilization that sustains the state against indigenous rebels").[65] In his reply, Governor Navarette declared Cenotillo excluded from the concession made to the criadores de ganado. He instructed that those who had already created these crías de ganado should move to the area previously fixed for the establishment of livestock. Authorities in Espita carried out Navarette's orders, and on 23 October 1863 the president of the junta municipal of Cenotillo ordered livestock owners to move their cattle within forty days to a location where they could establish the crías de ganado according to the law of 23 November 1844.

The alacrity with which the government responded to Canché and Cabrera's petition can be attributed to the political scenario of the times and provides a window into the instability of the period 1858–63. These years, which on the national front were occupied with liberal reforms under Benito Juárez that principally broke down corporate landholding, had a very different impact on Yucatán. Here the period was marked by instability and civil war, with the governorship changing hands no less than six times. One of the main developments of this time was the growth of antigovernment forces in the eastern pueblos of partidos such as Espita and Valladolid, where Caste War hostilities were intensifying. Government liberals such as Liborio Irigoyen, safely nestled in Mérida, seemed to be lost in their own petty interests and did not appreciate the escalating tensions on the frontiers. Corruption and self-interest also meant that the government in Mérida was now disappointing more and more people, chief among them the soldiers whose payments were no longer reaching them on time. The Oriente revolt—as the rebellion of the eastern communities came to be known—in fact started in Cenotillo in 1859, though it was not until 1862 that Felipe Navarette, a wealthy scion of the Espita-Valladolid area, would wrest power and augur in a new phase of conservatism in Yucatecan politics. The main agenda of the Oriente rebels had been the reprioritizing of the Caste War. Navarette believed that resources had to be reassigned to address the continuing hostilities. Once in power, he proved eager to please his supporters in the eastern partidos. As Rugeley writes, "The strongman suffered from the inability to say no, a syndrome common to those anxious to consolidate their new power by granting favors."[66] Cenotillo had been a crucial support base for Navarrete, and it was probably his desire to please his supporters there that prompted him to respond favorably to Canché and Cabrera's request.

How representative were Angelino Uicab and Andrés Canché's cases of the struggles of other nonrebel caciques in the Caste War era? Certainly each case is unique and the details of each different. In 1851, the cacique Juan Pascual Poot of Yaxkukul, for instance, was dismissed from office without the knowledge of the government in Mérida after he came into conflict with the juez de paz of the town over the latter's exploitation of indigenous labor.[67] After his dismissal, juez de paz José Silviera replaced Poot with Silviera's own servant, José María Tun.[68] It was not until a cholera epidemic led to the death of most of the república de indígenas and the lack of a wartime cacique became especially problematic that Poot was reinstated.[69] Each case is different in its details and outcome, but a unifying thread runs through all of them: the critical importance of the cacique's relationship with local government officials during the war. As well, in all cases caciques acted as political figures challenging the power of abusive jueces or, as in the case of José María Tun, colluding with them. And in this respect, I would argue that Canché and Uicab's stories speak to the experiences of many other "ordinary" caciques in the Caste War period.

Canché and Uicab's life stories also show that caciques continued to make alliances across racial lines even during the height of the Caste War. Uicab allied with a vecino of Mérida, Enrique Manzanero, as well as the juez Gregorio Lara. Interracial alliances also held the promise of ameliorating the hardships faced by indigenous communities in the wake of the fighting. Canché's alliance with Comandante Cabrera proved to be critical not only in making the cacique an important figure in his community but also in defending the interests of Cenotillo's indigenous community.

CHAPTER 5

"Your Majesty Loves the Indians"

The Defensor and Maya Commoners in the Years of Maximilian's Empire

When Empress Carlota appeared in Mérida in late November 1865, she was greeted by a throng of admirers. The empress looked demure in a white dress with blue trimmings and a matching hat. As she stood on the balcony of her apartments, she apologized to the crowd below for the absence of Emperor Maximilian and remarked with good humor, "He deeply regrets he cannot be here with me. . . . He will regret it still more when I inform him of the enthusiastic reception you have given me." Throughout her journey in Mexico, Carlota met with signs of acceptance of the empire under Maximilian. On her return journey from Yucatán, she was offered breakfast by a poor indigenous woman. When Carlota sat down to the simple meal, the old lady spoke: "I like Your Majesty very much, because you are very good, and because you have an Indian lady of honor, which proves that Your Majesty does not dislike, but rather loves the Indians."[1]

Adulatory accounts of Empress Carlota's visit to Yucatán abound. Although these sometimes contained exaggerations, it is nevertheless true that the years of Maximilian's empire (1863–67) in Mexico were a departure from previous regimes, especially in terms of government relations with indigenous people. Faced with the daunting task of becoming accepted in a new country, Maximilian set out to befriend the masses—in Yucatán this meant the Maya commoners—introducing a legal representative, the *abogado defensor de indios*, whose main task was to ensure the wellbeing of indígenas. As the defensor began his work, he traveled into interior villages of Yucatán listening to the complaints of the poor Maya population. Though he left behind a huge paper trail, there was only so much the defensor could accomplish. Practical limitations and the reality of imperial bureaucracy meant that his contributions were too little, too late. Ultimately the defensor's importance lay not in his actions but rather in the hopes that his presence raised among Maya commoners.

Whereas Maya caciques had engaged in political alliances with government officials since at least the late colonial period, in the 1860s Maya commoners would engage in their own experiments with clientelism. As the power of repúblicas began to wane, these people looked to other institutions for alliance. It would not be until the 1870s that debt peonage tied the Maya into relationships with hacendados from which they would find it difficult to escape. The 1860s thus presents the liminal period when indígenas would begin to be incorporated into hacienda life but from which they could still leave if they took advantage of the new legal measures instituted by Maximilian's empire. As Maya commoners now began their own politics of "petty paternalism"[2] by seeking favors from the newly installed defensor, they could for the time being escape the pressures of hacienda life and abuses of local officials such as jueces. Now also for the first time since independence, they could bypass their own caciques and present their grievances directly to the defensor. The years of the empire would thus represent the last gasp of Maya commoners as they experienced the possibilities of competing alliances—with the cacique, the hacendado, and the government in the person of the defensor.

EXIGENCIES OF EMPIRE

In late 1861, France, Britain, and Spain began to enter Mexican territory with the overt desire of forcing Mexico to pay its monetary debts to these European countries. The Second French Empire seemed, however, to have a much larger agenda: taking control of Mexico itself. In 1863 a military expeditionary force under the French entered Mexico and took control of the capital, Mexico City. In October of that year, the crown of Mexico was officially bestowed on the Archduke of Austria, Maximilian Ferdinand, who now became Emperor Maximilian I.

Although conservatives in Mexico hailed the return of monarchy as a victory, Maximilian, despite being the emperor, did not share completely in conservative views of how Mexico should be administered. In fact, Maximilian had a far more liberal outlook. For instance, he refused to acquiesce to conservative demands to suspend the liberal reform laws and return church properties seized by Benito Juárez. As the head of a monarchy, which had replaced almost a half-century of republican rule, and being a foreigner, Maximilian needed above all to bring legitimacy to his rule. Through his emphasis on creating a broad support base among the masses, Maximilian hoped to achieve this legitimacy and to present himself as a benevolent ruler to his newly conquered people. This showed itself in his desire to create a peasant base of support for his monarchy. The *comisario imperial* of Yucatán, Salazar Ilarregui, tried to "cultivate peasants" by introducing the figure of the defensor abogado, who would now represent the needs of indigenous people in the region.[3]

The years of the empire represented a fundamental reversal of the relationship between the legal system and indigenous people. Throughout the pre-empire years of the post-independence period, law in most cases had played a circumscribing role with regard to indigenous people. For example, laws related to literacy disenfranchised many indígenas, and vagrancy laws made it a criminal offense to be "lazy." Under the empire, in the role of the defensor came an official whose main duty was to represent the interest of indigenous people. In many ways this position harked back to the days of colonial rule. In its purpose it was reminiscent of the post of the protector which had been instituted in the early colonial period by Spain. The post of the protector had had its origins in the idea that indígenas were minors whom it was the job of the protector to defend—a patronizing idea, to say the least.[4] In certain ways, the post of the defensor worked on the same premise. The defensor was responsible for all cases involving Maya peasantry, including hearing their complaints, filing petitions, and representing them in court.[5]

The history of the defensor mainly resides in two persons who held this post. The first, Joaquín Patrón, held this post till 1864 and less is known about him. The second, José Demetrio Molina, was an accomplished lawyer, and his cases in Yucatán are the primary basis of our discussion here. Accounts left by Molina himself as well as other extant documents give us a detailed account of his activities as defensor and provide us a unique glimpse into the life of indigenous communities during the years of the Second Mexican Empire.

HACIENDAS AND THE CHANGING LANDSCAPE OF YUCATÁN IN THE 1860s

One the biggest changes to the Yucatecan landscape in the nineteenth century was the burgeoning of haciendas. The henequen haciendas—which harvested agave fibers for twine and rope—would reach their apogee late in the century, with Yucatán becoming the country's richest state in the 1880s, but by the 1860s the haciendas were already established in Yucatán.[6] To say that the haciendas altered the spatial landscape of Yucatán in this time would be an understatement. In fact, by the 1860s the rapid growth of haciendas had brought about fundamental changes in Yucatecan society that were felt most deeply by the rural and indigenous populations. One of the consequences of the hacienda economy was the number of indigenous people who became associated with haciendas as laborers and peons. By the beginning of the 1860s, Maya society was divided, with a growing segment living in haciendas disconnected from indigenous communities. Especially in the northwest districts of Yucatán, where haciendas were the most developed, the percentage of indigenous people living in haciendas was almost half of the total indigenous population. In 1862, for instance, 42 percent of indigenous residents of the district of Mérida were living on haciendas.[7]

Henequen haciendas in particular were labor intensive and often required laborers to live on the hacienda year round. The laborers who worked as peons on haciendas conducted their entire lives within their boundaries—working there, establishing families, and even spending their money in the infamous hacienda stores.[8] It seems clear from parish registers that these peons were seen not simply as workers but as members of the hacienda community. Though many peons had originally left their indigenous communities to join the hacienda workforce, according to government censuses and birth/death registration records these persons were no longer officially part of the indigenous communities. In the census of Izamal in 1851, for instance, the residents of the pueblo of Izamal were counted separately from hacienda residents.[9] In the eyes of the census office, there was a separation between the world of the hacienda and the world of the pueblo. Arguably, this separation had deeper social consequences, splitting the indigenous world.

The lives of hacienda peons were inextricably tied to the owners of haciendas. The hacendado had power over not just the peon's labor but over his familial relations and even his freedom of movement. A peon needed permission from his *amo* (master) before he could marry, and his children essentially passed into the power of the hacendado. A peon could not simply pick up and leave. The mechanisms of the hacienda, including the hacienda store—where workers could buy necessities for credit—and the hacendado's practice of paying taxes on behalf of the peons, ensured that they remained constantly in debt to him. To move from a hacienda and take employment elsewhere a servant had to produce a *carta cuenta*, a letter issued by the master certifying that the servant had no debts to the master and could freely take up other employment. Thus the main way that hacendados held on to their servants was through debt peonage. This can be seen, for instance, in a case from 1863 of a servant, Manuel Tus, along with his two sons, who left their master, hacendado Juan José Mendez, and took up employment in the hacienda of Don Gregorio Reyes. Mendez alleged that the servants had left without his issuing them a carta cuenta and that by law they should return to his hacienda. He also claimed that he had paid the religious taxes for the Tus children to the cacique of San Sebastián and thus the Tus family was indebted to him and, hence, bound to return to his service.[10] Not surprisingly, the mechanisms that kept a hacienda servant indebted to his master ensured that getting a carta cuenta was extremely difficult and, for certain individuals, almost impossible. This complicated relationship between servant and master would come out forcefully in the cases presented to the defensor.

THE DEFENSOR AND THE AMO

The year 1865 marked the first time in the national period that a state-appointed official visited pueblo after pueblo listening to indigenous people, hearing their complaints, and trying to resolve them. On 9

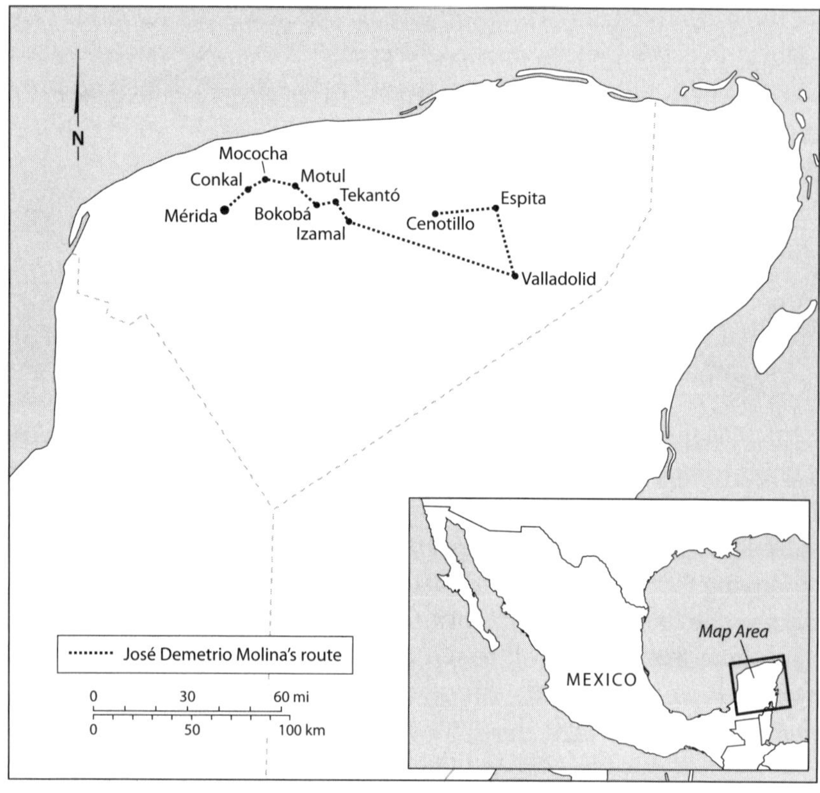

José Demetrio Molina's 1865 journey through Yucatán. Map by Bill Nelson. Copyright © 2017, University of Oklahoma Press.

January 1865, the abogado defensor José Demetrio Molina set off for what can only be described as one of the most interesting journeys in the history of Yucatán. In this journey, Molina traveled through Conkal, Mococha, Motul, Bokobá, Tekantó, Izamal, Valladolid, Espita, and Cenotillo before returning to Mérida via Izamal.

Although Molina traveled with his own entourage—including an assistant (the *defensor auxiliar*) and probably an interpreter—his journeys were partly organized by government officials. Thus, prior to Molina's stop at Valladolid, the juez de primera instancia of Valladolid had already sent an announcement to all the pueblos of the partido that Molina would arrive in Valladolid, thereby advising both locals and people who lived farther from the city that they could come and present their complaints or cases to him.[11]

The numerous cases Molina heard from residents of haciendas are testament to the impact of haciendas on indigenous life. Many of these complaints concerned questions of labor and debt, but we also encounter indígenas approaching the defensor to seek amelioration of personal, family situations. A recurrent *queja* (complaint) both in this journey and in cases brought generally to the defensor was brought by hacienda workers who wanted to leave their current masters and go elsewhere for employment. The infamous carta cuenta thus became a persistent theme in cases dealt with by the defensor, on a daily basis.[12] Many indígenas sought a carta cuenta not simply to take different employment but to escape the abuses of the present master. This can be seen, for instance, in a case of one Gervacio Xiu, who had worked as a *cochero* (coachman) for Estanislao Cámara. In Mérida in October 1865, Xiu complained to the defensor auxiliar that his master was mistreating him.[13] The defensor auxiliar discovered that Cámara was abusive to other servants too, demanding money from them if they missed work. After getting physicians to certify that Xiu was suffering from tuberculosis and needed to work in less strenuous jobs, the defensor auxiliar represented Xiu against his amo and ultimately the juez primero de paz ordered the amo to release the carta cuenta. In another instance, Eleuterio Chalé, an indigenous resident of hacienda San Rafael, sought the help of the defensor to mitigate the abuses of his master, hacendado Don Gumesindo Ruiz.[14] Chalé had been confined to a cell for two days by Ruiz and then whipped on Ruiz's orders. The defensor again championed the cause of Chalé, and the poor man was eventually set free.

Keeping a worker indebted was at the heart of peonage since it bound a peon to the hacienda indefinitely. However, even workers who were not indebted peons faced similar abuses from their amo. In March 1865, hacendado Joaquín B. Vargas demanded that the indígenas Francisco Koyoc, Juan Ventura Chan, and Juan Cetz return to his service in hacienda Balche, located in Izamal.[15] Vargas claimed that the three men had promised him to work on his hacienda for the entire agricultural year starting in July and were legally bound to honor their commitment. The defensor auxiliar, José María Osorno, took up this case, representing the indígenas. He argued that the law of 13 May 1847, which was still operational, did not define the time in which a laborer could leave a hacienda. As long as a laborer had done the work that he had been paid for and was not indebted to the hacendado, he was free to leave. In addition, the defensor auxiliar noted that, given the abuses suffered by the indígenas at the hands of this particular hacendado, they already had enough reason to leave his service. This would not be the last time that the defensor auxiliar crossed paths with Joaquín Vargas. In November 1865, another indígena named Aniceto Chim would bring charges against Vargas, accusing him of physically abusing him through whipping and incarceration.[16] Once again Osorno as defensor auxiliar took up Chim's defense.

Settling disputes over debts also occupied the defensor's time. On his journey through the Oriente (East), the defensor's first stop was the town of Conkal, east of Mérida. Here Molina followed up on a case pending from the time of the previous defensor, Don Joaquín Patrón, and required Don Gervasio Aranda to pay back a sum of money he owed an indígena named Luciano Cian. In another case, on 21 August 1864, the defensor along with José María Osorno appeared before the juez primero de paz representing an indígena named Juan Crisóstomo Chablé against one José de los Angeles Ortega. In this case, the defensor used documents as proof to demand that Ortega pay a sum of twenty pesos, which he owed Chablé.[17]

In addition to issues of labor and debt, Molina represented indigenous people against their hacendados on more personal matters. In Valladolid, José María Cab appealed to Molina, complaining that Don Eligio Rosado refused to give the license to his servant Narcisa Sen to marry Cab.[18] Molina responded by requesting the prefecto to ask Rosado to send the license. When Rosado failed to respond, Molina asked the prefecto to follow up on this case, highlighting a limit on Molina's ability to resolve disputes. His involvement in cases, especially during his trip, allowed him only a brief time in which he could actively defend an indígena. The necessity of the journey—to cover as many pueblos as he could in a short amount of time—meant that there simply was not enough time for Molina to bring resolution to cases. He had to rely on the imperial bureaucracy in the person of officials such as the prefecto to act in his place.

Even when the parents left a particular hacienda, the hacendado often tried to keep their children. Though ostensibly acting as guardians of servant children, it is undeniable that the hacendados used these children as servants on their property.[19] In the Second Empire, indigenous people could reclaim their children by appealing to the defensor. It is not surprising, therefore, that one of the most frequent types of case dealt with by Molina was that involving issues of guardianship by hacendados. During his month-long journey, Molina's stop in Valladolid was one of the busiest on his itinerary. There he met María Catarina Balam, an indigenous woman who complained that Doña Soledad Rosado (presumably the ama of Balam) was holding her daughter María Marta Chí.[20] The situation was particularly complicated if the parents died and the child was left orphaned and powerless to resist the hacendado. In 1865 the defensor was presented with just such a case concerning a young Maya boy named Tiburcio Yam.[21] Yam's father worked on the hacienda Funis in the pueblo of Kanasin as a servant of hacendado Don Joaquín Castellanos. After his father died, leaving him an orphan, Tiburcio Yam came under the power of Castellanos. For reasons that are not clearly mentioned in the documents, Yam at some point left the hacienda of Castellanos and traveled to Ticul, a distance of almost fifty miles. In Ticul, we are told, he came under the power of Don Pastor Medina. The defensor entered the case as a representative of Tiburcio Yam, who wanted to name Medina as his legal guardian in place of Castellanos.

Having workers live in haciendas, marry, and have children effectively served the purpose of reproducing the labor force in haciendas. *Luneros* (literally "Monday workers") had existed as an available pool of labor since the colonial period. As communities lost land to private estates, indigenous people became luneros in neighboring haciendas. In exchange for use of water, firewood, and hacienda land, luneros worked as nonsalaried laborers one day a week.[22] Luneros were usually also assigned to cultivate twenty mecates of land for the hacendado, although they could cultivate more at their own discretion. By 1843, however, this class of once-free peasants had become indistinguishable from debt peons, and by 1858 luneros were the most numerous class of servants on Yucatecan haciendas.[23] In March 1865, a Maya woman named Carmen Ek appealed to the defensor to gain custody of her daughter.[24] Ek's husband had been a lunero on the hacienda owned by Josefa Mesa. At some point Mesa had taken Ek's daughter, Lugarda Baas, to work for her. This had all taken place many years ago and yet, even after all this time, Josefa Mesa refused to return the daughter to Ek. Molina took on the case and was successful in representing Carmen Ek, with the final result that Josefa Mesa received orders from the secretario of the juez de primera instancia de lo civil, Mauricio Tejeres, to hand over the girl to her mother.

In protecting indigenous interests, Molina came into conflict with vecinos other than hacendados. The practice of holding on to indigenous children seems to have been widespread among wealthy vecinos. In a case that would continue for almost a year, an indigenous woman, Manuela Balam, appealed to the defensor to help her get custody of her daughter, who was being held by Doña Micaela Zetina.[25] Balam was the servant of Doña Saturnina Guillermo. Micaela Zetina was the sister of this Saturnina and on the basis of this relationship had taken Balam's daughter. In representing Balam, Molina argued that as the mother of the child Balam was better suited as a guardian than Zetina, since no one could provide better care than a mother. In this Molina was breaking new ground. Throughout the early national period the government had continued to see indigenous people as minors and inferior to vecinos. The government view (as expressed in the law of 27 August 1847) was that indigenous people needed to spend time in "tutelage" before they could become citizens. By asserting that Balam was a better guardian than Zetina, Molina was in effect challenging this view. This case would not come to a close in 1865; it was not until May 1866 that the case was finally resolved, in favor of Balam and the defensor.[26]

The huge number and varied types of cases involving hacienda indígenas that Molina fought to resolve demonstrate that beleaguered servants were quick to take advantage of the legal option of the defensor to ameliorate their situation. Having struggled over labor, indebtedness, custody of children, and other issues arising out of their situation as hacienda servants, these indigenous people finally had a government official to voice their complaints to, and someone who would take their side.

THE DEFENSOR: RESOLVING INTERNAL PROBLEMS OF INDIGENOUS COMMONERS

Although the defensor and his auxiliar represented numerous indigenous men and women in their struggles against their vecino masters, several documents including court cases show that the defensor was involved in resolving internal disputes among indigenous people as well. This was obviously a significant change from the functions of previous local officials, whose only interest in indigenous life had been ensuring the efficient and timely collection of taxes. Perhaps even more surprising is that indigenous people went to the defensor to resolve their internal cases, demonstrating an unprecedented degree of trust in the legal official and perhaps also some hesitation to rely on an indigenous leader such as a cacique. Indigenous commoners saw alliance with the defensor as a new way to ameliorate their situations and to gain individual favors or benefits.

In June 1866, the defensor Molina became involved in a case of child custody between parents. The wife, Andrea Ceh, complained that her husband, José María Dzakol, had abandoned her and her son eight months earlier. Now, after so many months Dzakol was attempting to gain custody of his child.[27] Molina was caught in a quandary; as a defensor of indígenas he was supposed to protect the interest of both parties. The case ended with Andrea Ceh and José Dzakol declaring that they would live together in the future. In another case of child custody during his journey, in Izamal, Molina was responsible for removing Francisco Balam from the guardianship of his mother, who was declared to be senile.[28]

Along with child custody, another issue that preoccupied Molina was inheritance. Through Molina's efforts in Mococha, one of the earliest stops in his journey, the executor of Manuel Valle's will was asked to show his accounts of the estate so that the assets of the deceased were divided among his four heirs, including José María Cetz, whom Molina was representing.[29]

Molina also on occasion resolved questions of inheritance of livestock.[30] In June 1865 in Mérida, Molina appeared before the juez de paz Lic. Don Manuel R. de León; he was representing an indígena,

Lázaro Ek, in a *juicio verbal* (oral trial) against his neighbor Doña María Herrera.[31] The properties of Ek and Herrera were adjacent, separated by only a short wall. The problem arose from the fact that Herrera's livestock was entering Ek's *solar* (garden plot). The final verdict was that Herrera was given one month to raise the wall between her house and Ek's solar or pay the latter to get the wall built. Molina also represented indígenas over questions of property and land rights. In October 1865, several residents of the town of Chicxulub appealed to the defensor to help them establish the boundaries of sitios Copo and Chan Pich, which belonged to them.[32] The sitios lay within the pueblo of Chicxulub, and these indigenous residents wanted their *mojoneras* (landmarks) to be defined officially so they would protect their property from any kind of encroachment. In response, the defensor had a surveyor go to the sitios and clearly demarcate their boundaries. In both cases, the defensor protected the properties—whether livestock or land—of Maya commoners who sought his help. These cases also demonstrate that the defensor ultimately depended on other bureaucrats and officials—in these cases the jueces de paz and surveyor—to fulfill his mission to represent the interests of the Maya population.

THE DEFENSOR AND THE BUREAUCRACY

The advent of the empire brought with it new government officials, such as prefectos and subprefectos and, of course, the defensor. This did not, however, mean the end of the old bureaucracy of pre-imperial years. In some cases, members of the old bureaucracy such as jueces and jefes continued in office and became the new prefectos and subprefectos.[33] There was thus a great deal of continuity between the old and new government officials. Also quite evident from existing documents is that in many areas the offices of juez, jefe, and others from the old republican days were not phased out. Rather, we see in document after document a coexistence of government officials from both the old and the new bureaucracy. The superimposition of the two sets of bureaucracies would have important implications for the defensor, and in many cases his success would depend on coopting or allying with these officials. The occasional breakdown of this uneasy marriage between the old and new official systems can also be seen in several cases involving the defensor and would prove to be one of the major limitations on the defensor's ability to achieve his goals of representing indigenous people.

Old habits die hard and throughout the imperial years we find instances of jueces abusing their power over the indigenous population. And, consistently, the defensor emerged time and again to champion the rights of this subaltern group. One of the earliest examples comes from a document from 1864, when the defensor was Don Joaquín Patrón. In October 1864, Patrón acted as the defensor abogado of indígena María Francisca Baas.[34] In this case, Patrón claimed that the juez de paz of Kanasín had ruined (surely an euphemism for "raped") Baas's daughter Juliana Can and then handed her over to the *mayordomo* (steward) of the hacienda Sihunchen. Patrón declared that this had been an illegal action on the part of the juez and that he had no justification for taking the girl from her mother. Patrón asked the juez segundo de lo civil to immediately instruct the juez of Chocholá to take the daughter from the mayordomo and hand her over to her mother.

In 1865, José Demetrio Molina replaced Patrón as the abogado defensor and followed in the footsteps of his predecessor by taking on a case of several indigenous residents of the town of Yaxkukul against the juez de paz of the town, Bernabé Molina.[35] The defensor represented Cayetano, Marcelino Chan, and Hilario Uc, who alleged that the juez had forced the villagers to give him a large sum of money and three horses. In addition the juez had incarcerated them for resisting forced labor. Of course, jueces abusing indígenas, extorting money from them, and putting disobedient indígenas in jail was nothing new. What was new and surprising was that another government-appointed official—here the defensor—was ready to call the juez out and demand that justice be done. The defensor's desire to uphold justice even if it meant going against a juez can also be seen during Molina's 1865 journey when he made a stop in the town of Bokobá. Here he was approached by the town juez de paz, who alleged that an indígena named José María Moo had usurped community land that had been part of the hacienda Soon.[36] With characteristic alacrity, Molina began an investigation into the case. When he found documents in Izamal showing that the land had been handed over to Moo legally, Molina was not shy to declare that the juez's accusations were unjust.

As defensor, Molina often had to depend on other government officials to resolve a case. In his final report upon the completion of his 1865 journey, Molina wrote that in the space of fourteen days he had visited twenty villages and towns and attended to the complaints of twenty-five pueblos. The huge expanse of the Yucatán peninsula and the multitude of problems presented to him every day meant that he could not administer justice as quickly as the claimants hoped for. In fact, because of the sheer volume of cases, Molina sometimes had to abandon one case to follow up on another. To solve this problem, his predecessor Patrón had made some complainants appeal in front of the juez de paz, and if the case was not particularly problematic or did not need the presence of the defensor to be resolved, then the juez was given the task of resolving it. Thus, government officials such as jueces were critical to the resolution of many cases. These jueces often had better knowledge of the areas under their administration, and they also had considerable authority bestowed on them.

The dependence between defensor and jueces created occasional conflict and posed limits on the defensor's ability to protect the interests of indigenous people. This can be seen in an 1865 case in which Molina tried to resolve a dispute between two indígenas, Pablo Pech and Andrés Mutu.[37] Molina claimed that Mutu was holding Pech's son and asked that he be returned to his father. When the juez José María Vado did not give the verdict that Molina hoped for, the defensor took steps to challenge the juez. He requested the juez to hand over all the documents pertaining to the case, since he wanted to appeal this decision. The juez chose not to comply with this request, stating as his reason that he was too busy with certain other criminal cases. At this stage, Molina, clearly exasperated, appealed to a higher government official, the juez de primera instancia de lo civil, Saturnino Juárez, to put pressure on Vado to hand over the documents. The latter responded to Saturnino Juárez that he had not sent the documents to Molina because the appeal was still pending. Clearly, when the old bureaucracy—in the person of the local juez de paz—and the new imperial bureaucracy—in the figure of the defensor—rubbed against each other, the result was not always harmonious. That he could not achieve his aims because of the inaction of other government officials clearly irked Molina. This is another case that highlights the limits of the defensor's powers. In the end he was deeply dependent on jueces and other government officials in resolving cases.

Another case from 1865 illustrates the same problem. On 14 September 1865, Molina appeared before the juez of Mérida, Manuel R. de León, and alleged that Don Andrés Urcelay had forced Estanislao and Abrosio Tec to work on his hacienda without pay.[38] Molina asked that Urcelay be ordered to release the cartas cuentas to the Tecs so that they could leave his hacienda and find employment elsewhere. In response, Urcelay testified that both the Tecs were indebted luneros and were doing personal service. Urcelay rejected the allegation that he had not paid the Tecs and claimed that there was not enough reason to give the carta cuentas to these two workers. In the final judgment on this case, the juez ruled in favor of Urcelay, saying that he saw no cause to separate the servants from the amo. In this case we see a difference of opinion between the juez and the defensor leading to a judgment that did not go Molina's way. The defensor had to cooperate with jueces, but this held the possibility that justice—at least in Molina's eyes—could be thwarted.

Perhaps one reason for the divergence of opinion between Molina and other officials was historical. Unlike the defensor, these older officials such as the jueces had never seen themselves as champions of indigenous people. Rather, throughout their experience as local authorities the jueces had often allied with powerful members of society and seen their indígena constituents as sources of labor and taxes, given to drinking and needing to be disciplined and kept in line. In particular, the Caste War years had created a sense of panic and distrust of indígenas among all levels of vecino society. It is not surprising, then, that these officials did not share Molina's ardor to protect indígenas.

In many cases the presence of government officials such as jueces was essential in *juicios* (trials), which could lead to complications when the juez and defensor could not agree on a verdict. But the defensor's dependent relationship brought other problems as well. Indigenous people saw the defensor as their champion and representative. In contrast, they sometimes feared members of the old bureaucracy. And though the defensor did represent indígenas in cases, he was not part of the local officialdom in villages; he mainly stayed in Mérida, and the point of contact between indígenas and the defensor was usually the courtroom. Maintaining a conciliatory relationship with their local jueces was of paramount importance to indígenas, since no matter the verdict of any one case, they knew they would still have to interact with these jueces on a daily basis. This often resulted in confusing testimonials by indigenous complainants. During his journey through the Oriente, Molina stopped in the town of Cenotillo, where he was approached by several servants of the hacendado Don Luis Ríos who pleaded with the defensor to help them get their carta cuentas.[39] Then, in a surprising about-face, these servants withdrew their allegations when they had to present their case before the juez. Instead, they confessed that they had been paid according to custom and had not been mistreated by their amo. Molina understandably dismissed this case upon hearing this testimonial, since there was no real reason in his eyes to justify release of cartas cuentas from the hacendado.

Working with other government officials and being part of the bureaucracy also had certain advantages for the defensor. Being an official himself, the defensor could appeal directly to the powers that be. During his journey, for instance, Molina visited Espita, where he was met with indígenas who complained that they did not have enough land to cultivate.[40] As a high government official, Molina was able to send a direct request to the governor of Yucatán asking him to cede a plot of land named Culnemax to the villagers.

At the same time, as Molina himself realized during his journey, dependence on bureaucratic channels could obstruct the efficient execution of justice. Though he continued his predecessor's practice of leaving certain cases for the juez to resolve, many jueces objected to this on the grounds that according to the law all interested parties had to be physically present at juicios verbales. In addition to the lack of enthusiasm among jueces to resolve cases involving indígenas was Molina's growing distrust of jueces themselves. In his final report at the end of his journey, Molina wrote that the lands named as ejidos had been given to indígenas by the Spanish crown for their use and sustenance; each indígena was to have sixty mecates of land to cultivate annually. According to Molina, the jueces of the pueblos took advantage of the indígenas' ignorance of this law to establish their patrimony over the communal lands, using the land themselves on a grand scale and leaving only the poorest lands to the indígenas. Molina claimed that some jueces had more than four hundred mecates of public land under their control and that, because of this abuse by jueces, the land of the pueblos was nearly exhausted. To solve some of these problems Molina recommended changes to the current legal setup, especially as it related to indígenas. In particular, he recommended that a special *Tribunal de Indios* be set up to deal with the question of indígena rights. Although this could in one sense be seen as an atavistic throwback to the colonial era when such tribunales de Indios had indeed existed in the Spanish American colonies, Molina's suggestion seems to stem from his frustrations with working with bureaucrats who clearly had contrary interests and aims when it came to defending indígena rights. The tribunal never really came into effect, but Molina's final report and, especially, his reflection on the role of jueces illustrate clearly the catch-22 situation in which he found himself—the dilemma of defending indigenous rights while depending on officials who prospered at the indígenas' very expense.

Practical issues also prevented the defensor from becoming a real part of indigenous life. Defensor Molina's hectic schedule meant that he often had to leave one case to take on another, in effect leaving unfinished business for other government officials such as the jueces to take care of. In addition, in the absence of a special tribunal dedicated to indigenous rights, Molina was woefully alone in his quest to protect the rights of the indígena population. In fact, although many indígenas appealed to the defensor to solve their problems, much of this was probably out of practicality rather than any feeling of real connection with the official. This is evident especially in cases where we see indígenas actually misusing or manipulating the defensor. Molina encountered his fair share of fortune hunters during his journey through the Oriente. In Pixoy, for instance, Dario Pech complained against Don Manuel Loria Esquivel for having usurped a land named Culunchacab.[41] No doubt Pech hoped that the defensor would take the land away from Esquivel and give it to him. In the end, however, the defensor realized that the assertion had been falsely made by Pech and the case was closed.

Despite being a champion of indigenous rights, Molina ultimately shared many attitudes with other vecino officials of the peninsula. This comes through in his final report where he writes, "The principal defect of the Indians is the profound indolence that stems from lack of civilization and from the excessive use of aguardiente."[42] This is perhaps not surprising given that Demetrio Molina was part of the Molina family and had also worked for the Peón family; both families would become the center of the wealthy henequen oligarchy in Yucatán under the Porfiriato.[43] In terms of worldview and attitude, the defensor was far closer to other government officials such as jueces de paz than his actions would suggest. It is thus important to view Molina not as some kind of "white legend" figure but as a bureaucrat who performed the difficult task of balancing indigenous interests with the inherent prejudices of the vecino class to which he belonged.

Over the course of the early national period, indigenous commoners—much like their caciques—learned to operate within the existing system by engaging in alliance making. However, this form of political behavior became best visible in the imperial period (1863–67). The coming of the defensor and with it a new layer of political authority provided a space in which we can see this politicization in action. In the person of the defensor, indigenous commoners for the first time had at their disposal a government official with whom they could ally. Mirroring cacique strategies of alliance with powerful government figures, we see indigenous commoners appealing to the defensor to remedy their individual situations in a kind of politics of petty paternalism. Rather than bargaining for communal or collective goals, the overwhelming political conduct here is one of securing individual favors. This new political situation where indigenous people could engage in alliance making without the sanction of their caciques or communities presented possibilities of political action in a post-república world. This period thus can be seen as the period of transition from "two republics to one divided," where such possibilities could be experienced and explored by indigenous commoners.[44] No doubt this experience would shape the expectations and behavior of indigenous commoners as the system of the two repúblicas, and with it, the cacique, would formally come to an end in the late 1860s.

CHAPTER 6

Of Promises and Dilemmas

The Defensor and Maya Caciques in the Years of Maximilian's Empire

Andrés Canché's political victory in having established a powerful alliance with military commander Buenaventura Cabrera and successfully defending the interests of indigenous commoners against cattle ranchers provided a fitting swansong for the aging cacique. On 14 November 1864, Canché submitted his resignation from the post of cacique.[1] He explained that after serving as cacique for thirty years (*"que hace el espacio de treinta años que desempeño en dicho pueblo el destino de cacique de su república de indígenas"*) he now wanted to step down because he was greatly afflicted by ill health, advanced age, and the need to attend to his own interests in order to sustain his family. Despite his age, Canché's signature at the end of his renuncia still retained its characteristic flourish, which bespoke a literate and Hispanicized individual. On 15 November, the *subprefecto político* of Espita, Pedro Rosado Lavalle, wrote to the prefecto superior supporting Canché's petition and confirming its veracity, and on 17 November Valentin Canché's name was proposed to replace the outgoing cacique.[2] The end of Canché's formal reign as cacique also coincided with one of the most important turning points in Mexican history. Felipe Navarrete's conservative victory as governor of Yucatán would segue into the beginning of Maximilian's empire in Mexico.

Empress Carlota's 1865 journey through Yucatán proved to be one of the high points of Maximilian's reign. As she embarked on this trip, Maximilian sent her instructions: "When inviting landlords always to include the village headman and leaders of the Indian deputations."[3]

In fact, Carlota's visit to Yucatán gave unprecedented importance to caciques. Terry Rugeley's account of the visit highlights how she carried out these instructions and gained the loyalty of Maya community leaders: "But the most remarkable moment of the tour happened in a remote town named Becal, and it was an event without precedent in Mexican history: the town's batab met the Empress, the only known occasion in which a Maya of that ancient title stood before the Mexican head of state. . . . The batabs pledged their loyalty to Carlota and in return received her blessing."[4] Maximilian's desire to achieve acceptance among all sections of Mexican society, and especially the rural peasantry, manifested itself in this unprecedented show of benefaction to the indigenous caciques. Yet Maximilian did not just espouse overt friendliness to the caciques and indigenous communities. Rather, he instituted new legal measures to foster a relationship of mutual support and alliance, chief among them being the installation of the abogado defensor. This would have contradictory results, especially for caciques. Though to some extent the defensor would serve to protect indígena rights and help caciques to represent their communities, it would also undermine the caciques' power.

Yet the coming of the empire did not mean the end of the previous era. Under the empire the highest official was the *comisario imperial* (imperial commissar). Under the comisario imperial was the *prefecto político,* who was responsible for large administrative areas and macro-districts, and below him was the *subprefecto,* who was responsible for local administration and smaller subdistricts. The defensor was a separate official whose main function was to represent indígenas in legal cases. The old bureaucracy, with its officials such as the jueces de paz, entered into an uneasy coexistence with these new officials, a coexistence that sometimes dissolved into outright conflict.

There is no doubt about the salience of continuities into this imperial period; Rugeley, for instance, notes that that the "imperial years offered no abrupt departure from what came before or after."[5] Nevertheless, documents related to the defensor shows that there were very real changes that indigenous people, including caciques, experienced under the empire. Legal aides had always been available to indigenous people, but the defensor represented a fundamental reformulation of the relationship between the state and indigenous people. Though in general indigenous leaders and indigenous people welcomed the changes, the coming of the defensor proved to be both a boon and a curse for the caciques. Caciques were now called on by the defensor to present their complaints and concerns to him, but their own authority in village matters could now be undermined.

With the coming of empire, the indigenous repúblicas themselves had declined in importance. It is true that years of war and the effects of the growth of haciendas had combined to create a sense of impoverishment and weariness. But there is also a sense in the archival documents that Maya people no longer saw serving in the repúblicas as lucrative or desirable. It is also likely that they were apprehensive of how the new regime would affect them. Indeed, the year 1864, which saw Canché's resignation from office, witnessed numerous other cases of indígenas contriving one or another excuse to escape duty in the indigenous repúblicas. Echoing Canché's retirement, in December 1864 Luciano Pech of Temax requested to be relieved of the post of cacique after serving thirteen years because his old age no longer permitted him to do his duties; in the same month, Sixto Koh, teniente of the república de indígenas of Temax, also filed his resignation, again citing old age and poor health as the reasons.[6] On 30 December 1863, Romualdo Abad of Izamal requested the government to excuse him from serving on the indigenous república to which he had been nominated because the injuries he had suffered while in military service during the Caste War had left him "*inútil*" (useless).[7] In January 1864, Marcelino Mex of Acanceh complained that he had over the years served in various capacities in the república—as alcalde, regidor, and teniente. Now he had been chosen as the *tupil* (constable) of the república. Mex requested the government to relieve him of this charge so that he could look after his family.[8]

In many ways the dynamics of rural life had changed. Many indígenas now earned their living not through their milpas but in the employ of richer vecinos. On 29 July 1864, José Santiago Piste of Kantunil requested the prefecto to excuse him from serving on the república because of his ill health and because he was already occupied as an indebted servant in the employ of Don Luis Ríos.[9] In December 1864, José Irineo Ek of Izamal asked to be excused from serving as regidor of the república because he was already employed as a servant in a large family.[10] In 1865 the cacique of Santa Ana had proposed the name of José María Cuá to serve as regidor of the república de indígenas. Cuá, however, was already employed as a cochero to Antonio Bolio, who refused to release him to take up the position in the república.[11] The proliferation of such cases suggests that by the time the emperor began his brief rule, repúblicas no longer offered the prestige or lucrativeness they once held. Whereas even in the early decades after independence indígenas had vied to control the repúblicas, now that was no longer the case. Canché's resignation thus reflects the general Maya apathy with the repúblicas in the 1860s.

To some degree the Caste War was certainly responsible for the apathy; it had weakened indigenous communities and caciques, even those who remained loyal to the government. Moreover, this decline was not simply a top-down affair; rather, we see instances of the cacique's loss of legitimacy at the local level. Part of this decline can be attributed to the rise of haciendas as competing bodies to the indigenous communities. The high number of hacienda indígenas appealing directly to the defensor to resolve problems suggests that these indígenas no longer saw the cacique as their legitimate representative. Other instances of indigenous commoners complaining against their cacique serve to add to the picture of the waning power and legitimacy of caciques even before the formal abolition of the post of cacique in 1869. At the same time, the imperial era allows us to see how the forms of political conduct normalized by caciques over the early national period shaped the forms and aspirations of peasant politics as Yucatán transitioned from "two republics to one divided."

Interestingly, the two main breaks in the post-independence landscape of Yucatán—the Caste War and Maximilian's empire—both proved essential in helping the cacique survive in his formal position until it ended in 1869. It was the exigencies of war that led to the formal restoration of caciques and their repúblicas in the law of 27 August 1847. The government even doled out honorific hidalgo titles to reward and retain loyal caciques. Similarly, under Maximilian, one of the tenets of government was that, in Rugeley's terms, "batabs and repúblicas would maintain their accustomed authority."[12] It is likely that the tendency of liberal governments to chip away at the corporate power and privileges of indigenous repúblicas would have resulted in the abolition of these bodies and their caciques much before 1869 if these two historic events had not intervened.

Although the post of cacique was abolished by the end of the decade, the story of the 1860s is not simply a story of failure of this office. Rather, we see caciques continuing to defend their communities, entering into alliances with government officials old and new, and trying to use all available means at their disposal to remain in power. The 1860s was therefore a critical period for Maya caciques and commoners: it was a time of new hopes stirred, new allies made, and new struggles fought.

CACIQUES: CONTINUITIES AND CONSTRAINTS IN THE IMPERIAL YEARS

Many indígenas saw the coming of the empire almost in a millenarian fashion. They felt that the establishment of monarchy would reverse the wrongs of the previous half-century and restore to them long-lost privileges. In particular, indígenas believed that with the coming of empire the land that had belonged to them at the time of Conquest would revert back to them. But if the coming of the defensor felt like a godsend to indigenous commoners, the experience of caciques was more ambivalent.

The imperial years signaled both continuity and change for caciques. As far as caciques were concerned, the years of the empire did not completely erase the problems of the past. Renuncias of cacique positions thus continued as before. The main difference now was that new officials became involved in these renuncias. In April 1865 it was the newly created official subprefecto político who submitted the resignation of the cacique of Ticul and proposed the name of another indígena, Francisco Meña, to replace him.[13] The main reason given for the cacique's resignation was that he was sick and also illiterate. In fact, sickness continued to be one of the main reasons, at least ostensibly, for caciques to resign their post, as shown by the renuncia of Ignacio Cetzal in 1864. Cetzal, cacique of Espita, renounced his post because of bad health that was preventing him from fulfilling his duties as cacique and also causing detriment to his own agricultural interest, which was the only way for him to sustain his family.[14] Thus, the coming of the empire did not signal any real change in the economic and social hardships faced by caciques.

One of the main continuities between the pre- and post-imperial years was the complex relationship caciques continued to have with government officials. Instances of caciques allying with certain jueces and favoritism on the officials' part remained prevalent. Jueces often tried to replace caciques they did not get along with. In Tixkokob, for instance, the jueces de paz complained to the prefecto político against the cacique José María Poot, citing his continuous drunkenness as the reason for replacing him with their candidate, Aniseto Cauich.[15] Another case from the pueblo of Sitpach illustrates this tendency toward favoritism. On 1 October 1865, José María Nauat and Anselmo Cocom complained to the prefecto superior against the juez auxiliar, Alcocer.[16] Nauat claimed that he had been the rightful cacique of Sitpach and Cocom his teniente. According to Nauat and Cocom, Alcocer had concocted a false list of cacique and república leaders to be elected in Sitpach, which caused Nauat and his teniente to be removed from office. Nauat and Cocom also asserted that there had been a massive protest among indígenas in their pueblo after the naming of the other cacique. As this case shows, jueces would resort to even illegal measures such as falsifying names of república leaders in order to displace caciques who were not allied to them and replace them with ones who were.

Although alliances with certain jueces continued, caciques also had to interact with the new bureaucracy brought into place by the coming of the empire. Alliance between officials and caciques was, of course, a two-way street, and we find examples of caciques championing certain officials of the new order. This can be seen, for instance, in a case from September 1864 from the town of Tizimín, where the cacique Anselmo Dzul defended the subprefecto's treatment of indígenas.[17]

A cacique's relations with local government officials also colored his relations with his community. In July 1864 we find that the juez de paz of Cansahcab, Teodosio Canto, joined the cacique of the town to appeal to the governor to demarcate common lands, possibly to thwart hacendados who had begun to encroach on them.[18] In certain cases, these officials also defended caciques when their own communities turned against them. This can be seen in the case of the town of Timucuy in January 1864.[19] Here indígenas complained to the governor that their cacique, Ignacio Canul, forcibly made them work and also engaged in illicit relations with their wives. The indígenas made this *denuncia* (complaint) with the hope that they could replace this cacique. The jefe político of the partido, however, immediately came to the cacique's defense, explaining that he was not as cruel as the villagers portrayed him. Rather, the jefe averred that it was the cacique's rigor in collecting taxes that had angered the community. The jefe admitted that Ignacio Canul had the habit of drinking but pointed out that it would be impossible to find any indígena in the pueblo who didn't.

Other cases of communities denouncing their caciques also make their way into the archives. In August 1864, the village and república of Espita appealed to the prefecto superior to replace their cacique, Nasario Cetzal, with another indígena named Felipe Tuc, because Cetzal had been working for private interests and not in the interests of the community.[20] The establishment of the office of defensor in particular not only allowed communities to bypass caciques and appeal directly to the defensor but also enabled them to voice their rejection of caciques altogether. In an interesting twist, the clientelism, which caciques had engaged in since the late colonial period to hold on to power in the face of exclusionary state policies, had now percolated to the peasantry, with the poorer classes seeking favors and alliances from those in positions of power.

Such cases also point to the increasing importance of private interests in village life, especially as it related to caciques. As we have seen, by the 1860s private capital especially in the form of haciendas had burgeoned, and hacendados were constantly empowering themselves at the expense of indigenous communities. The rise of haciendas had important consequences for caciques. We know that poverty and sickness mired the lives of many caciques in the 1860s. A natural consequence was caciques allying with private interests in order to secure themselves financially. A document from 1861, for instance, shows the cacique of Cacalchén, Juan Xool, working for a hacendado and in debt to him.[21] This kind of dependence created conflicts of interest, and this was something that the government was aware of. Xool's dependence on the hacendado as well as the fear that he would not be able to manage his duties led to his dismissal from the post. A similar case can be found in Calotmul, where the cacique Juan Baas worked as an indebted servant to the hacendado Patricio López.[22] Once more, the cacique here was removed because of his dependence on the hacendado.

Even when caciques remained independent of haciendas, their lives were intertwined with those of hacendados, and not always in positive ways. One reason for this was that caciques continued to collect taxes into the 1860s. In many villages, hacendados still carried on the practice of paying taxes for their resident peons (using this later to bind them into indebtedness).[23] Thus, caciques had to interact with hacendados at least during the times of tax collection. Indeed, before the coming of the defensor, the cacique was often the main champion of indigenous communities against exploitative hacendados.[24] It is likely that in whatever small way caciques probably continued to shield their communities from hardship. Indeed, caciques continued to intervene on behalf of their communities on questions of land and labor. As noted above, in 1864 the cacique of Cansahcab allied with the juez de paz to defend the common land against a hacendado's encroachment. As another example, also in 1864, the cacique of Cacalchén asked the government to exempt certain indígenas of his community from fagina duty.[25]

While caciques continued to represent and defend their communities, in certain ways actions of the empire undermined their authority and privileges. Sometimes, for instance, laws that were meant to assimilate caciques into the structure of administration worked against their interests. In 1866, the *comisario municipal* (municipal commissar) included the name of Gregorio Sosa, cacique of Chicxulub, in the list of public functionaries. For generations, caciques had reaped the reward of being seen as separate from other officials because of their indigenous status. But after being categorized as a public official, Sosa was dismayed when the government slapped him with taxes that all other functionaries paid.[26] This case highlights the ambivalent impact of the empire on caciques. Actions that conferred prestige on the cacique (e.g., by positioning him as a public official) also weakened certain traditional privileges. The imperial years also saw a greater sense of cacique accountability. Punishment for caciques seen to be dishonest or exploitative was sharp and immediate, as in the case of the cacique of San Sebastián, Bernabé Canché, whose properties were seized by the government when it became known that he had been expropriating money from public funds.[27]

The grand visit of Empress Carlota to Yucatán had signaled to caciques that their power would grow under the empire. In practice, however, imperial policies often undercut cacique power, as in the case of the cacique Agustín Chan of Chablekal.[28] In March 1866, Agustín Chan complained to the prefecto político of Yucatán against the comisario municipal of Conkal. Chan wrote that he had given orders to certain indígenas of his pueblo to work on some repairs in the public jail. One indígena, Euán, did not comply with this order, so the cacique punished him by giving him the task of laying a road for a certain distance. However, when the comisario municipal heard about this, he reprimanded Chan in front of the indígenas and told him that he could no longer punish any indígena of the república. Moreover, the comisario municipal found out that Chan had given some money (presumably public money) to certain indígenas for voluntarily working on some lands. The comisario ordered the cacique to pay back to the comisario all the money that he had distributed.

This case is interesting because it shows unprecedented imperial constraints on caciques. Whereas in the past caciques had always assigned community members to certain tasks and even, informally, punished them, they no longer were seen as having the right to act in such a way. The comisario's actions may have emerged from the heightened sense of indigenous rights prevailing among the new officials (such as the defensor). Here, by punishing the indígenas the cacique had—in the eyes of the empire—contravened their rights. Ironically, it was only by undermining the traditional rights of the cacique as a leader of the indigenous community that the comisario could hope to resolve this issue. By castigating Agustín Chan in front of the indígenas of the pueblo, the comisario effectively undermined his authority, and by forbidding caciques from punishing indígenas or distributing money to them, imperial officials were undercutting the long tradition of cacique governance of pueblos.

THE CACIQUE AND THE DEFENSOR

When the defensor Demetrio Molina made a stop in January 1865 in Cenotillo, he was approached by the aging and penurious Andrés Canché, cacique of Cenotillo. Canché complained to Molina that, although he had long served the government, he was now reduced to poverty and could not take care of his family. As a result of Molina's intervention, Canché would receive help from Cenotillo's indigenous commoners, who agreed to sow fifty mecates of milpa to help sustain him.[29] Toward the end of his life, the rebellious cacique of the 1830s had mellowed, realizing that survival depended on making powerful friends. It was surely a sign of the times that the indígenas ultimately agreed to sow the cornfield not at the request of their longtime cacique but at the behest of the new government functionary.

Of all the innovations of the imperial years, the one that affected caciques most directly was the installation of the office of the defensor abogado de Indios. In certain ways the coming of the defensor proved to be a positive development for caciques. In certain cases they were able to appeal to the defensor and get his help in ameliorating the condition of their communities. This can be seen, for instance, during Molina's journey through the Oriente when caciques of the repúblicas of Valladolid complained that the indígenas in the city of Valladolid were obligated to work at the hospital and were not paid sufficiently; women were paid only two reales per week and men only four reales.[30] Molina responded by raising the salary to one peso (eight reales) per week plus food for men and four reales plus food for women. Like other indígenas, caciques could also use the services of the defensor for personal benefit. In the town of Ebtún, the cacique appealed to the defensor to get a sum of money owed to him by a man named N. Fernández.[31]

As the account of Molina's journey shows, caciques from repúblicas far and wide came to speak with him and present the grievances of their communities. In that sense, the defensor was an ally, and a powerful one at that. However, sometimes this could turn against the cacique. For instance, it was on the basis of a report made by the defensor that the cacique of Caucel was replaced in December 1864.[32] Caciques too could present their complaints to the defensor, but this was a double-edged sword. The defensor could help the cacique in redressing wrongs, but he could also report deviant behavior on the part of the cacique to the government. It turned out that way when the cacique of Uayma complained to Molina that several landowners had established rancherías in the montes of the community without paying rent. In resolving and reporting this issue, Molina laid part of the blame on the cacique: "I won't let it go without saying that this issue has been caused in part by the indigenous leader of that town, when he started out, he leased out those lands, without any right to do so, making use of the products of his rentals, in any way that he wished, with the rest of the indígenas."[33] According to Molina, this abuse introduced others whereby vecinos from other pueblos started cultivating the land and paying rent at certain times and not at others.

In other cases, Molina took it on himself to intervene in the conduct of caciques. In the town of Ebtún, for instance, a man named Luciano Noh complained to the defensor that the cacique forced him to work in public projects despite his old age and poor vision. Molina immediately took action against the cacique and asked the juez to order the cacique to not disturb Noh, since his infirmities were visible enough.[34]

There was another level of complication in the relationship between caciques and the defensor. Caciques from the colonial period onward had established alliances with local government officials in order to bolster their own power and legitimacy. These alliances were based on personal relationships often forged over time through daily interaction at the local level. Although the defensor was a government official, there was a real distinction between him and other officials such as jueces. Unlike these officials, the defensor was not a part of local networks of power. He briefly sojourned through a few towns but had neither the longtime association with pueblos nor the personal relationships on the ground that other local government officials had. Thus, for caciques the defensor represented an anomalous entity who could come to the localities and represent indigenous people but at the same time remained outside the pale of local networks. This circumstance made the possibility of any real long-term alliance between caciques and the defensor (in contrast to many alliances that caciques formed over the years with officials such as jueces and alcaldes) virtually nil.

Moreover, though the defensor held a great degree of authority, caciques were not equally happy in welcoming him. This can be seen even during Molina's journey when he stopped at Espita to meet with the indigenous leaders of that town. In the beginning the leaders of the indigenous república would not trust him, and Molina had to convince them that he was the legitimate defensor before they decided to voice their appeals to him.[35] Caciques also sometimes regarded the defensor as an outsider and refused to cooperate with him. The cacique of Muxupip, Gerónimo Pat, for instance, refused to hand over documents to Molina that he needed in order to help peasants of Muxupip in a case of land litigation with the neighboring pueblo of Euán.[36] As this case also suggests, there was probably a sense of power struggle between caciques and the defensor, and it is important to raise the question: did the defensor replace the cacique in localities?

DID THE DEFENSOR REPLACE THE CACIQUE?

Despite facing impoverishment in his old age, Andrés Canché continued to remain involved in local politics. On 23 May 1865, a year after resigning from office, Canché once again joined hands with Buenaventura Cabrera, this time against the jueces of Cenotillo.[37] Cabrera and Canché alleged that, despite orders issued by the government in October 1863, the jueces of Cenotillo were again establishing crías de ganado in ways that negatively affected residents of the town. Despite the fact that the petition was signed by the new cacique, Valentin Canché, there is no doubt that the petition was drawn up by Andrés Canché and Buenaventura Cabrera. In fact, although this is the final case file in the archives in which Andrés Canché appears, he seems to have remained associated with the case, with officials assigned to resolve the case approaching him for information on it.

By the early 1860s, the Caste War had again turned hot. By 1865, Cenotillo had begun to feel the effects of the revived hostilities. In fact, reports from December 1865 suggest that Cenotillo had been invaded by rebels and sacked.[38] With the military in residence, tensions in villages and towns were bound to burst forth. Cabrera's continuing disputes with owners of livestock and his petition against the jueces are perhaps expressions of the tension that inevitably arose with competing authority figures jostling for control in the localities. That Andrés Canché, despite having left his post as cacique, should remain involved in formal petitions also leads to interesting inferences. It is perhaps not entirely a coincidence that one of the jueces denounced in the petition was none other than Felipe Correa. This juez had instigated the 1855 case against the then lone cacique. But now in 1865, armed with a powerful alliance, Canché was the figure on the offensive. Even if Canché was acting purely for the interests of his community, revenge must have felt sweet. The fact that he remained associated with this case despite being out of office also points to his continuing legitimacy as the voice of the pueblo and his enduring power as an influential figure in Cenotillo. Canché's involvement in the case also attests to the strength of his relationship with Cabrera, who was prepared to maintain a long-term alliance with the ex-cacique even when the latter had retired and been left with no legal authority. In Canché's case, then, caciques continued to remain at the forefront of community struggles despite the installation of the defensor.

Despite being accountable to the defensor when he visited their town, the caciques continued as before in administering their villages. In some ways the defensor himself was reliant on the caciques for his own success. As practically an outsider to indigenous communities, the defensor had to depend on the cacique to make sure that the indígenas of pueblos remained industrious and "yield a surplus with which to advance themselves . . . and above all . . . moderate their use of aguardiente, which is the main cause of all their quarrels and missed obligations."[39] Indeed, caciques continued to intervene in questions of land and labor in their communities.

Coming through in the documents is an almost clear separation of cases handled by the defensor from those resolved by a cacique. By the 1860s there seems to be a division in the indigenous world between indígenas living in the community and indígenas living in haciendas. The defensor deals mostly with cases concerning individual indígenas in struggles with their hacendados; the cacique mostly intervenes on behalf of the indigenous community as a whole, rather than for particular individuals. Although there is some overlap, this holds true most of the time. This suggests that more hacienda workers appealed to the defensor because they felt that they did not have a communal claim on the cacique's services. In the cases where the cacique confronted the hacendado, it was mainly to protect the interests (whether related to land or labor) of the members of the indigenous community. Thus, although both the defensor and the cacique represented indígenas, in some senses they were not stepping on each other's toes. Of course, these boundaries were not always clear-cut, especially when indígenas belonging to the community worked as luneros on haciendas.

Although the defensor did not replace caciques, he did undermine their status in several ways. With the coming of the defensor, indígenas could appeal directly to him and bypass their cacique. In some cases, the defensor would take over land litigation cases that had previously been administered by the cacique. If the defensor found a cacique abusing authority or acting in an undesirable manner, he could complain to higher authorities. And caciques were subservient to the defensor in the chain of power and were expected to carry out instructions from him. Thus, although at the start of the empire we see caciques being invited by the Empress Carlota herself and being shown respect and fealty, the actual mechanisms that came into play to some degree served to undermine the power of caciques in certain towns and villages. At the same time, caciques like Andrés Canché continued to act as local political figures, challenging the power of abusive jueces and engaging in strategic local alliances.

POST-EMPIRE

The Second Mexican Empire in Yucatán came to an end in 1867. With the new federal republic, time seemed to speed up, and changes in indigenous life suddenly began to occur in leaps and bounds. By

January 1869, the system of separate repúblicas officially came to an end and the post of cacique was abolished. Immediately, ayuntamientos in towns and villages began the process of dismantling the physical markers of the old república system. Municipal authorities in Telchac, for instance, sought the government's approval to rent out the portion of the *casa real* (a public building sometimes used as an inn for travelers) that had previously been occupied by the república de indígenas.[40] The years of the empire had seen heightened activity on the part of the government to protect indigenous rights through legal mechanisms, and it seems likely that this would have alienated the hacendado class as well as officials such as the jueces de paz. Whether this alienation among the planter and official class contributed to the new republican government's desire to enact quick changes and ensure elimination of indigenous rights is a subject of speculation. In any case, it is clear that—at least officially speaking—the cacique post died a quick death even before the end of the decade.

Although no longer present in an official capacity, in practice those who had been caciques continued to remain important leaders in their communities. The government had decided to abolish the repúblicas, but clearly caciques were still indispensable to maintaining order among the indigenous masses. Thus on 31 December 1868, the government in Mérida outlined a new role for ex-caciques: they were to remain for the moment as *auxiliares de las autoridades* (assistants to the authorities) for maintaining order among the indígenas.[41] Recalling their past services and their habitual ability to manage the indigenous classes, the government declared that until new legal mechanisms were set up these men would serve as organs of communication between the authorities and the indigenous people. It is interesting to note that, even as the government was planning the abolition of the post of cacique, it continued to see these local figures as the only legitimate intermediaries between itself and the indígenas. A year after the abolition of the post of cacique and the repúblicas, in December 1869, pueblos of the partido of Motul were still busy creating lists of propertied Maya (undoubtedly including ex-caciques) who could function as alcaldes auxiliaries in their respective towns and villages.[42]

Ayuntamientos, which eventually took over the work of indigenous repúblicas in most pueblos, also continued to interact with and depend on those who had been caciques. This can be seen in a case from the town of Hunucmá.[43] In 1871 a resident of that town, Eleno Basto, had declared a piece of land as baldío. Declaration of a land as baldío was usually a prelude to appropriation of the land by private interests. In this case, the declaration was followed by a tumult among indígenas who denied that the land was baldío and claimed that they had already paid for measuring and demarcating it. The ayuntamiento, which had not authorized this payment of money or measurement of land, now approached the once cacique of Hunucmá, Juan de Dios Col, who had served in the position in 1868. Col explained to the ayuntamiento that he had collected the money from the village at the instruction of the jefe politico for measuring the land and delivered the money to him in 1869. Thus, we see the case of a man continuing his cacique functions after the position of cacique had been abolished and well into the 1870s. He was the first person the ayuntamiento approached to clarify the dispute, and it was based on information the cacique gave the ayuntamiento that in 1875 the council could order the jefe politico to hand over the money the villagers had paid for land demarcation.

The continued visibility of previous caciques in their villages had both positive and negative results. On the one hand, as the above example shows, it could help the ayuntamiento resolve certain cases involving the villagers and meant that the ex-cacique continued to be a powerful presence in the community. But it also meant that he remained publicly accountable for his actions even after legally he had ceased to occupy his post.

For Maya commoners the years of the new federal republic brought little or no reprieve from the daily travails of life. They continued to face harassment at the hands of the rich and powerful—but now without recourse to caciques, repúblicas, or the defensor for help. In 1872, for instance, Maya peasants in Teabo were drafted into forced labor in ranches by the authorities of their town.[44] In 1871, indígenas in Tahmek found themselves in prison when they resisted being forced to work for the jueces de paz of the town.[45] Like caciques before them, Maya commoners too sought patron-client relationships as a means of survival. That they would find them mainly in the institution of peonage on the burgeoning henequen haciendas would be one of the ironies of the new post-república world.

Conclusion

> The oldest hath borne most: we that are young
> Shall never see so much, nor live so long

The year 1865 is the last we encounter Andrés Canché in archival records. Yet the years between 1834 and 1865 provide a fascinating glimpse into this extraordinary figure. In Canché we see a quintessential cacique whose life provides a window into local politics in early national Yucatán. We find, for instance, the centrality of cacique relations with local government officials in the aftermath of the municipal revolution and establishment of ayuntamientos; it was antagonistic relationships with the alcalde that led to Canché's dismissal from office first in 1836 and then again in 1855. In Canché, we also find a cacique who was able to use to his advantage even difficult circumstances, such as the coming of the Caste War. Apart from gaining the support of the governor by remaining loyal, Canché formed meaningful alliances at the local level that made him a powerful player in local politics; despite the repeated attempts by the juez de paz and cura to oust him, Canché continued to return to his post until he himself renounced it in 1864. Canché's alliance with Buenaventura Cabrera in particular helped him gain local power and defend communal interests. Well into the 1860s, Canché remained active in defending communal lands from usurpation by livestock raisers.

Despite his powerful alliance with Cabrera, Andrés Canché seems to have derived his legitimacy from his community. We know that he served as cacique only from 1834 to 1836 and then again from 1852 to 1863 with a possible break of a few years starting in 1855—a total of less than thirteen years. Yet Canché's own actions and words show that he saw himself as the cacique of Cenotillo regardless of whether he held the official post. In 1837, more than a year after being relieved of duty, Canché wrote to the governor referring to himself as "cacique of Cenotillo" to complain against subdelegado Manuel Elizalde. In his letter of resignation in November 1864, Canché wrote that he had served as cacique for the past thirty years, thereby including in his tenure the years in which he had officially not held the post. That Canché continued to see himself as cacique even after 1864 can be attested by the fact that he presented himself to Molina as cacique of Cenotillo in 1865. Canché's actions suggest that his view of himself as cacique did not depend on government sanction but rather that he derived his self-identity from his association with his community. This comes through clearly when we see Canché continuing to defend the interests of his community against the invasion of livestock haciendas in May 1865.

The story of Andrés Canché also illuminates a paradox: as caciques became powerful local figures, they also became more dependent on government officials. At the end of his life, Canché remained important to his community and involved with communal land struggles, but we see a breakdown of values of reciprocity whereby Canché could no longer derive support from the community for his own sustenance. Rather, in 1865 Canché had to ask the defensor to order the indigenous people of Cenotillo to sow corn for his sustenance. The defensor Molina in effect became the intermediary between the cacique and his community. As the years progressed, even the most independent-minded cacique had to find benefactors to survive.

By the end of the early national period, the successful cacique was a client cacique. To be economically, socially, and politically influential, the cacique needed powerful vecino allies. These friends or patrons usually came from the ranks of government officials assigned to localities where there was the highest likelihood of frequent contact with the cacique. Indeed, power at the local level came from personal relationships cultivated through interactions during daily activities, which the cacique had to coordinate—distribution of labor, collection of taxes, and upkeep of the public buildings, among others. Whereas it had been his position in the community and the república and his role as mediator between the vecino and Maya worlds that had provided the cacique power and legitimacy since colonial times, by the end of the early national period this was no longer the case. With increasing authority in the hands of local officials such as jueces and alcaldes, being a simple intermediary was no longer a sufficient source of power. After all, with the exception of tax collection, nearly all administrative power was now in the hands of local officials.

Still, historical events contrived to maintain the importance of the archaic role of cacique as mediator. During the Caste War the cacique's ability to mediate with his community suddenly became of paramount importance as the state sought to create a loyal countryside. In the chaos and paranoia of the rebellion, only those caciques who the state saw as loyal—as a client—retained their positions and, in some instances, their lives. Indeed, throughout the 1850s and 1860s power and survival depended on patronage in one form or another—whether by state officials, military authorities, or the church. To be sure, the state had never envisioned that caciques would ultimately use the new system to their advantage. In repeatedly legislating to retain caciques but with limited powers and privileges, the state had overlooked that at the local level this very powerlessness would impel caciques to find novel ways of inserting themselves into the process of governance. The tools the caciques used were the same ones that the state employed to keep the villages under control: the local officials. Over the years caciques tapped into this resource, forming alliances with local authority figures until clientelism defined the narrow village politics of post-independence Yucatán. As these alliances became the source of power, the repúblicas began to matter less—not just to caciques but to the Maya commoners as well. The reluctance to serve on repúblicas was just one way this new dynamic of rural politics revealed itself. There were now more powerful people—hacendados, for instance—and institutions to tie oneself to other than the waning repúblicas. That the indígenas of Cenotillo ultimately agreed to help Andrés Canché by sowing his cornfields had more to do with their desire to please the abogado defensor than from any lingering sense of loyalty to the cacique.

But was this transformation superficial? A glance through the wills and testaments of indígenas suggests that by the end of the early national period the wealthy and successful indígenas were also the most Hispanicized. When Manuel Koyoc, cacique of the suburb of Santiago in Mérida, died in 1858, he left behind an enormous fortune—property worth almost two thousand pesos.[1] Koyoc was a devout Catholic, and his possessions included a statue of the Virgin encrusted with silver and pearls and a rosary of gold and coral. Apart from leaving property to his wife and children, he also left behind an intriguing legacy: a sum of money to the Biblioteca General de la Nación, that is, the national library. It is possible to imagine that Koyoc had visited this library in his lifetime, a mark not only of being educated but of being comfortably part of the urban vecino world. Koyoc's other bequest, to the hospitals in San Lazaro and San Anton, also marks him as a rich and distinguished Meridano. Koyoc even had several Maya servants working for him to whom he left individual legacies. But there is nothing in this will to indicate that Koyoc was Maya. Indeed, but for his Mayan name Koyoc could very well have passed for a successful vecino with all the cultural traits of that class.

Not as rich as Koyoc but still fairly well off, José de La Cruz Moo of Kopoma passed away in 1865.[2] Like Koyoc, Moo's most precious possessions were those that demonstrated his faith: a rosary of pure gold and a crucifix with a silver crown. But the most striking aspect of Moo's last will and testament was not his bequests but his instructions for his own burial: "*Que mi cuerpo sea enterrado en el cementerio comun, con exequias de infima clase.*" He asked to be buried in the common cemetery with the funeral rites of those of the lowliest classes. It is almost as if in death Moo reclaimed his place among the downtrodden Maya—those of the lowliest class. Moo's burial instructions evoke the image of the *común*, the Maya common lands that had once been the heart of indigenous rural life.

Perhaps at the end of the early national period in Yucatán, for every Koyoc there was a Moo—for every acculturated Maya, an indígena who sought his final resting place among the familiar echoes of the past.

Notes

Abbreviations Used in the Notes

AGEY	Archivo General del Estado de Yucatán
AGN	Archivo General de la Nación (Mexico)
CAIHY	Centro de Apoyo a la Investigación Histórica de Yucatán
PE	Poder Ejecutivo
vol.	volumen (volume)
exp.	expediente (file)

Introduction

1. James Lockhart, *The Men of Cajamarca: A Social and Biographical Study of the First Conquerors of Peru* (Austin: University of Texas Press, 1972).

2. Akhil Gupta, "Blurred Boundaries: The Discourse of Corruption, the Culture of Politics, and the Imagined State," in Aradhana Sharma and Akhil Gupta, eds., *The Anthropology of the State: A Reader* (Hoboken, N.J.: Wiley-Blackwell, 2006), 220.

3. The MLA is an elected representative to the legislature of a state and the BDO is an official appointed to oversee the operations at the block level (one of the subdivisions of local governance) in India.

4. For works that look at indigenous and subaltern participation in Latin American state formation in the independence and early national periods, see Peter Guardino, *The Time of Liberty: Popular Political Culture in Oaxaca, 1750–1850* (Durham, N.C.: Duke University Press, 2005); Eric Van Young, *The Other Rebellion: Popular Ideology, and the Mexican Struggle for Independence, 1810–1821* (Stanford, Calif.: Stanford University Press, 2001); Charles Walker, *Smoldering Ashes: Cuzco and the Creation of Republican Peru: 1780–1840* (Durham, N.C.: Duke University Press, 1999); Brooke Larson, *Trials of Nation Making: Liberalism, Race and Ethnicity in the Andes, 1810–1910* (New York: Cambridge University Press, 2004).

For works on the contemporary period, see Gilbert Joseph and Daniel Nugent, eds., *Everyday Forms of State Formation: Revolution and Negotiation of Rule in Modern Mexico* (Durham, N.C.: Duke University Press, 1994); Marisol de la Cadena, *Indigenous Mestizos: The Politics of Race and Culture in Cuzco, Peru, 1919–1991* (Durham, N.C.: Duke University Press, 2000); Florencia Mallon, *Courage Tastes of Blood: The Mapuche Community of Nicolás Ailío and the Chilean State, 1906–2001* (Durham, N.C.: Duke University Press, 2005); Deborah Yashar, *Contesting Citizenship in Latin America: The Rise of Indigenous Movements and the Postliberal Challenge* (Cambridge: Cambridge University Press, 2005).

5. Timothy Mitchell, "Society, Economy, and the State Effect," in Sharma and Gupta, *Anthropology of the State.*

6. Paul Friedrich, "The Legitimacy of a *Cacique*," in Steffin Schmidt et al., eds., *Friends, Followers and Factions: A Reader in Political Clientelism* (Los Angeles: University of California Press, 1977), 275.

7. Liberalism's negative impact on indigenous self-government can also be seen in other parts of Mexico in the nineteenth century. Andrés Lira examines the ambivalence of the Mexican state toward indigenous repúblicas (known as *parcialidades*) in his case study of Tenochtitlán and Tlatelolco. Lira also shows how indigenous communities allied with elite conservatives and that it was not until liberal policymakers gained control of the state that indigenous communities lost their wonted privileges. See Andrés Lira, *Comunidades indígenas en frente a la ciudad de Mexico* (Zamora: Colegio de Michoacan, 1983). For the impact of liberalism on indigenous communities in frontier areas, see Evelyn Hu-Dehart, *Yaqui Resistance and Survival: The Struggle for Land and Autonomy, 1821–1910* (Madison: University of Wisconsin Press, 1984).

8. Eric Wolf, "Aspects of Group Relations in a Complex Society: Mexico," *American Anthropologist* 58, no. 6 (1956), 1075, 1076.

9. James Lockhart and Stuart Schwartz, *Early Latin America: A History of Colonial Spanish America and Brazil* (New York: Cambridge University Press, 1983), 113.

10. Charles Gibson, *The Aztecs under Spanish Rule: A History of the Indians of the Valley of Mexico, 1519–1810* (Stanford, Calif.: Stanford University Press, 1964), 150.

11. Robert S. Haskett, "Living in Two Worlds: Cultural Continuity and Change among Cuernavaca's Colonial Indigenous Ruling Elite," *Ethnohistory* 35, no. 1 (1988): 34–59.

12. Gibson, *Aztecs under Spanish Rule*, 118, 196.

13. Greg Grandin, *The Blood of Guatemala: A History of Race and Nation* (Durham, N.C.: Duke University Press, 2000).

14. Sinclair Thomson, *We Alone Will Rule: Native Andean Politics in the Age of Insurgency* (Madison: University of Wisconsin Press, 2002).

15. Yanna Yannakakis, *The Art of Being In-between: Native Intermediaries, Indian Identity, and Local Rule in Colonial Oaxaca* (Durham, N.C.: Duke University Press,

2008); Alida C. Metcalf, *Go-betweens and the Colonization of Brazil, 1500–1600* (Austin: University of Texas Press, 2005).

16. Terry Rugeley, *Yucatán's Maya Peasantry and the Origins of the Caste War* (Austin: University of Texas Press, 1996).

17. Matthew Restall, *The Maya World: Yucatec Culture and Society, 1550–1850* (Stanford, Calif.: Stanford University Press, 1997), 63.

1. Setting the Stage

1. Unless otherwise noted, all primary documents referred to in this chapter's notes are from Ralph Roys, *The Titles of Ebtun* (Brooklyn, N.Y.: AMS Press, 1983).

2. An unusual characteristic of this collection is that it contains some documents written in Mayan, which are painstakingly translated for the reader. Most documents one encounters in the archives of Yucatán are Spanish-language documents written by Spanish officials. Although there are a considerable number of Spanish-language documents in *The Titles of Ebtun*, the presence of Mayan documents also allows us to hear the voices of indigenous people, or at least of the indigenous authorities, directly. At the same time, there are inherent problems (e.g., perspective, selection, interpretation) associated with any edited collection of translated documents. Nevertheless, the value of Roys's work cannot be overestimated.

3. Among scholars of Yucatán who have referred to the collection are Nancy Farriss, Matthew Restall, Robert Patch, Philip Thompson, and Pedro Bracamonte y Sosa. These scholars use the Ebtún documents primarily to discuss land disputes in the colonial period.

This chapter does not aim to provide a comprehensive review of caciques in the colonial period in Yucatán. Other scholars have already attempted this task, in particular, Sergio Quezada in *Maya Lords and Lordships: The Formation of Colonial Society in Yucatán, 1350–1600* (Norman: University of Oklahoma Press, 2014). For colonial Yucatan, Restall's *Maya World* and Robert Patch's *Maya and Spaniard in Yucatán, 1648–1812* (Palo Alto, Calif.: Stanford University Press, 1994) still remain some of the best sources.

4. Yucatán's experience contrasts with that of more core areas, such as Central Mexico, where Spanish control was much more direct and effective. See Susan Kellogg, *Law and the Transformation of Aztec Society, 1500–1700* (Norman: University of Oklahoma Press, 1995).

5. Restall, *Maya World*, 27, 38.

6. Patch, *Maya and Spaniard*, 68–72.

7. Matthew Restall, *Maya Conquistador* (Boston: Beacon Press, 1998), 49.

8. Nancy Farriss, *Maya Society under Colonial Rule: The Collective Enterprise of Survival* (Princeton, N.J.: Princeton University Press, 1984), 180.

9. Roys, *Titles of Ebtún*, 123.

10. Patch, *Maya and Spaniard*, 89.

11. John Lloyd Stephens, *Incidents of Travel in Yucatán*, vol. 1 (New York: Harper and Brothers, 1843), 196.

12. Philip Thompson, *Tekantó, a Maya Town in Colonial Yucatán* (New Orleans: Tulane University Middle American Research Institute, 2000), 38–39.

13. Quezada, *Maya Lords and Lordship*, 40.

14. Restall, *Maya World*, 79–80.

15. Ibid., 73.

16. Thompson, *Tekantó*, 49–51.

17. For a detailed discussion of the office of the protector, see Charles Cutter, *The Protector de Indios in Colonial New Mexico, 1659–1821* (Albuquerque: University of New Mexico Press, 1986).

18. For a detailed analysis of the legal system as it pertained to indigenous people in colonial Mexico, see Woodrow Borah, *Justice by Insurance: The General Indian Court of Colonial Mexico and the Legal Aides of the Half-Real* (Berkeley: University of California Press, 1983).

19. Farriss, *Maya Society*, 355.

20. Mark Lentz, "Assassination in Yucatán: Crime and Society, 1792–1812" (Ph.D. diss., Tulane University, 2009), 180.

21. D. A. Brading, *Miners and Merchants in Bourbon Mexico, 1763–1810* (New York: Cambridge University Press, 1971), 35.

22. Sergio Quezada, *Breve historia de Yucatán* (Mexico D.F.: Colegio de Mexico, 2001), 99.

23. Polushin found a similar dynamic of state officials increasingly interfering in local affairs after the Bourbon reforms in Chiapas. He emphasizes the symbiotic vertical bonds between indigenous leaders and subdelegados in Bourbon era Chiapas. See Michael Polushin, "Bureaucratic Conquest, Bureaucratic Culture: Town and Office in Chiapas, 1780–1832" (Ph.D. diss., Tulane University, 1999).

Some historians, such as Mark Lentz in "Assassination in Yucatán," suggest that the Bourbon reforms did not bring new people into the indigenous pueblos but rather new offices, with influential creoles continuing to be in positions of power.

24. Referring to the late colonial period, Terry Rugeley (*Yucatán's Maya Peasantry*, 35) writes that "previously Mayas had resisted the encroachment of large estates on village lands, but increasingly they found themselves in competitions with other peasants, villages with other villages. Hence, in the extensive records of Ebtún, a Maya village near Valladolid, one recurrent theme is the land dispute between Ebtún and the nearby village of Cuncunul."

25. This can be seen in 1764 when indigenous authorities gathered to reconcile the boundary map of Sotuta with those of Tekom, Cuncunul, and Tixacal, in Document 20, "Reconciliation of the boundary map of Sotuta," 1764.

26. Document 21, "Acknowledgment of the preceding document by Antonio de Arze," October 15, 1775.

27. Document 57, "Petition by the protector to restrain trespass," June 6, 1797; Document 58, "Order by the Governor for Manuel de Arze to investigate and correct trespass," n.d.

28. Document 60, "Report of survey of the north line," September 5, 1797.

29. Document 61, "Manuel Arze reports having warned the people of Ebtún," September 8, 1797.

30. Document 60; Document 62, "The protector petitions the Governor," September 25, 1797.

31. Document 63, "Decree by the Governor enforcing protector's request," September 25, 1797.

32. Document 65, "Ebtún petitions the Governor," n.d.

33. Document 25, "Acknowledgment of sale of the Tontzimin tract: Diego Chay to Diego Cupul," March 6, 1838.

34. Document 66, "The Governor forwards the preceding petition to the protector," December 2, 1801; Document 67, "The protector advises an examination of the map," December 3, 1801.

35. Document 69, "Report of the Subdelegate," December 16, 1801.

36. Document 70, "Cuncunul petitions the defender," n.d.

37. Document 76, "The Governor orders the sale of Tontzimin," February 15, 1802.

38. Document 75, "The opinion of the ministers of the exchequer," February 12, 1802.

39. Document 77, "Execution of the preceding decree by the subdelegate at Valladolid," February 24, 1802.

40. Document 81, "Report of the survey by Andrés Mariano Peniche," March 16, 1802.

41. Document 84, "The protector protests the legality of the survey," April 28, 1802.

42. Document 81.

43. Document 84.

44. Document 89, "The protector, in the name of Cuncunul, proposes that Tontzimin tract be divided," December 31, 1802.

45. The decree referred to is probably the decree of February 1802 ordering Cuncunul to sell the Tontzimin tract to Ebtún for twenty-five pesos. See Document 92, "The attorney general for the natives replies to the proposal to divide the Tontzimin tract," n.d.

46. Document 93, "The Governor refers the records to the lieutenant assessor," May 17, 1803.

47. Document 100, "Decree by lieutenant de Sandoval," ca. 1804–5.

48. Document 103, "Cuncunul petitions the defender general," n.d.

49. Document 105, "Don Juan Chan, governor of Cuncunul, agrees to drop the suit," July 19, 1812.

50. Document 108, "Ebtún petitions the defender for the return of documents," August 15, 1819.

51. Document 111, "The subdelegate remits the recovered documents to the Governor," September 2, 1819.

52. James Scott, *Weapons of the Weak: Everyday Forms of Peasant Resistance* (New Haven, Conn.: Yale University Press 1987).

53. Ranajit Guha, "The Prose of Counter-Insurgency," in Nicholas Dirks et al., eds., *Culture/Power/History: A Reader in Contemporary Social Theory* (Princeton, N.J.: Princeton University Press, 1994), 336–71.

54. Raymond Craib, *Cartographic Mexico: A History of State Fixations and Fugitive Landscapes* (Durham, N.C.: Duke University Press, 2004), 147.

55. Document 17, "Report of the survey made by Captain Antonio de Argaiz," June 14–26, 1700.

56. Document 22, "Minutes of the survey," October 15, 1775.

57. Document 64, "The subdelegate issues an order," October 5, 1797.

58. Document 82, "The subdelegate delivers the documents to Ebtún," April 3, 1802.

59. Document 92.

60. Mark Lentz (*Assassination in Yucatán*, 181) makes a similar point when he notes that the new bureaucratic layers made for more "convoluted proceedings, where Spaniards occupying different tiers of the power structure often found each other in opposition to one another, rather than uniting to subjugate the Mayas."

61. Document 22.

62. Patch, *Maya and Spaniard*, 162.

63. Kenneth Andrien, for instance, finds examples of corruption among subdelegados in the Andes after the Bourbon reforms. See Kenneth Andrien, *Andean Worlds: Indigenous History, Culture, and Consciousness under Spanish Rule, 1532–1825* (Albuquerque: University of New Mexico Press, 2001), 69.

64. Patch, *Maya and Spaniard*, 165–66.

65. Spanish entrepreneurs we encounter in the Ebtún documents include Gabriel Virgilio, who bought the Tontzimin tract from Diego Cupul and then sold it back to the community of Cuncunul in 1725.

2. Webs of Power

1. According to Carlos Alcalá Ferráez, Cenotillo experienced 35 percent mortality as a result of the cholera outbreak in the 1830s. See Carlos Alcalá Ferráez, "Cólera: mortalidad y propagación en la península de Yucatán, 1833–1834," *Letras Históricas*, no. 7, Fall 2012–Spring 2013: 115–41). For a detailed discussion of the role of cholera in state formation in Yucatán, see Heather McCrea, *Diseased Relations: Epidemics, Public Health, and State-Building in Yucatán, Mexico, 1847–1924* (Albuquerque: University of New Mexico Press), 2011.

2. AGEY, PE, Gobernación, caja 18, vol. 6, exp. 23, "Oficio del subdelegado de Valladolid, proponiendo terna para la designación del nuevo cacique de Cenotillo por haber muerto el anterior del colera morbus," 1833.

3. Carol Dumond and Don Dumond, eds., *Demography and Parish Affairs in Yucatán, 1797–1897: Documents from the Archivo de la Mitra Emeritense* (Eugene: University of Oregon Press, 1982), 32.

4. AGEY, PE, Justicia, Penal, vol. 15, exp. 21, "Causa seguida en el juzgado de Valladolid contra Andrés Canché y Feliciano Couoh por defraudadores de la hacienda publica," 1836.

5. Ibid.

6. Jordana Dym explores the importance of the municipalization process, albeit for Central America, in *From Sovereign Villages to National States: City, State, and Federation in Central America, 1759–1839* (Albuquerque: University of New Mexico Press, 2006).

7. Karen Caplan, *Indigenous Citizens: Local Liberalism in Early National Oaxaca and Yucatán* (Palo Alto, Calif.: Stanford University Press, 2010), 52–55.

8. Ibid., 106.

9. AGEY, Justicia, Penal, vol. 3, exp. 2, "Diligencias promovidas contra Francisco Chí, cacique de Izamal, por castigo de azotes que dio a José Rafael Chan y su esposa Juana María May a pedimento de Doña Francisca Bobadilla," 1825.

10. The Siete Partidas were first compiled under Alfonso X of Castile in the thirteenth century. They codified laws and established legal codes that remained in effect in Latin America for several centuries—in some cases well into the nineteenth century.

11. "Art. 191–Art. 208, Constitución Politica del Estado Libre de Yucatán," in Melchor Campos García, *Las constituciones historicas de Yucatán, 1824–1905* (Mérida, UADY, 2009), 322–25. According to Article 208 of the 1825 constitution, ayuntamientos were put in charge of maintaining public order in the pueblos, conserving the security of properties and persons of citizens, managing and investing wealth, promoting and caring for primary schools and hospitals, and building, repairing, and cleaning roads, prisons, and other public works. It was also their duty to form the municipal ordinances of the pueblo and submit them to Congress for government approval and to promote agriculture, industry, and commerce according to local needs and circumstances. On the literacy require ment, see Article 197, ibid., 323.

12. Caplan, *Indigenous Citizens*, 111, 117. Though the shift from federalism to centralism and vice-versa in Yucatán reflected the region's relationship to Mexican national government, in hindsight, as Terry Rugeley has pointed out (*Yucatan's Maya Peasantry*, 62–63), centralists and federalists are difficult to separate. Both parties comprised people with landed wealth, and the centralist leaders brought little meaningful change in agrarian policies vis-à-vis their federalist counterparts. The one significant change that Karen Caplan (116) has noted is that the centralist years brought more conflict into localities, especially with the installation of appointed (rather than elected) state officials directly at the local level.

13. Ibid., 112.

14. Terry Rugeley, *Rebellion Now and Forever: Mayas, Hispanics, and Caste War Violence in Yucatán, 1800–1880* (Palo Alto, Calif.: Stanford University Press, 2009), 25–29.

15. "Porfiriato" is the term used to denote the era of Mexican president Porfirio Díaz (roughly 1876–1911). The era was marked by modernization on the one hand and peasant impoverishment on the other.

16. AGEY, PE, Justicia, caja 25, vol. 4, exp. 27, "Información promovida por Bartolo Espadas vecino de Bokobá partido de la Costa, contra Don Olayo Barrera y Don Cecilio Sosa, alcaldes de Cacalchén y de Bokobá, por abusos de autoridad," 1840.

17. AGEY, PE, Gobernación, vol. 9, exp. 19, "Representación de Alejandra Ek, vecina del pueblo de Sotuta, pidiendo le sea entregado su hijo, del que fue despojado por el cacique de dicho pueblo," 1837.

18. Stephens, *Incidents of Travel*, 338.

19. AGEY, PE, Empleos, caja 14, vol. 2, exp. 54, "Representación de Macedonio Dzul, pidiendo se le reponga en su empleo de cacique del pueblo de Peto, al que se vio obligado a renunciar por presiones del anterior subdelegado," 1829.

20. AGEY, Justicia, Penal, vol. 15, exp. 44, "Diligencias promovido por Macedonio Dzul, vecino de Peto, contra el juez primero de dicho partido, por abuso de autoridad," 1836.

21. AGEY, PE, Gobernación, caja 17, vol. 4, exp. 20, "Copias certificadas de las actas levantadas en las diversas cabeceras por las juntas electorales de partidos, con la designación de individuos que concurrían a la elección de los diputados al Congreso General," 1832.

22. Rugeley, *Yucatán's Maya Peasantry*, 123.

23. Terry Rugeley, "Rural Political Violence and the Origins of the Caste War," *The Americas* 53, no. 4 (1997), 482.

24. AGEY, Justicia, Penal, vol. 45, exp. 48, "Causa instruida contra D. Cornelio Souza y D. Macedonio Dzul, cacique de Peto, por reunión tumultuaria y asonada," 1845.

25. Rugeley, *Yucatán's Maya Peasantry*, 98.

26. Karen Caplan (*Indigenous Citizens*) explains how the language and vocabulary of liberalism was appropriated by the local population to further their interests, in the process creating a multitude of "local liberalisms."

27. AGEY, PE, Gobernación, caja 17, vol. 5, exp. 14, "Expediente promovido por el C. Pablo Pérez, para comprobar las tropelías y abusos de autoridad del C. Joaquín Anguas, alcalde conciliador de Cauich, pueblo del partido de Lerma," 1832.

28. AGEY, PE, Justicia, caja 24, vol. 3, exp. 17, "Expediente promovido por Juan Antonio Keb y otro vecinos del pueblo de Nohcacab, contra Luciano Negro alcalde de dicho pueblo por atropellos en sus personas," 1832.

29. AGEY, PE, Justicia, caja 24, vol. 3, exp. 19, "Información promovida a petición de Juan Mepomuceno Lara contra Baltazar Baeza, alcalde de Kancabdzonot," 1832.

30. AGEY, PE, Gobernación, caja 17, vol. 4, exp. 18, "Expediente promovido por el C. Pablo José Pérez, contra el C. Benito Fuentes, alcalde conciliador del pueblo de Cantamayec, partido de Sotuta, por abusos de autoridad," 1832.

31. AGEY, PE, Justicia, caja 24, vol. 3, exp. 18, "Sumaria promovida a petición de Pantaleón Tinal, vecino de Tibolón contra José Manuel Avilés alcalde de Tabi por abuso de autoridad," 1832.

32. AGEY, PE, Gobernación, caja 16, vol. 3, exp. 20, "Representación de los indios del pueblo de Quelul acusando a Bernardino Jimenez, juez de paz de dicho pueblo, por obligarlos a torcer caña en condiciones injustas," 1831.

33. AGEY, PE, Gobernación, caja 16, vol. 2, exp. 4, "Copiador del decretos del año 1829 (incompleto)," 1829.

34. AGEY, PE, Justicia, caja 24, vol. 3, exp. 13, "Averiguación promovida por queja de los indígenas de Cholul, contra el juez de paz de Conkal, por violentarlos a desempeñar trabajos en las milpas del subdelegado, del cura y las suyas propias," 1831.

35. The *mecate* is a linear measurement of about 20 m; as a unit of area, one square mecate measures 400 m^2. Rani T. Alexander, *Yaxcabá and the Caste War of Yucatán: An Archaeological Perspective* (Albuquerque: University of New Mexico Press, 2004), 166.

36. Rugeley, *Yucatán's Maya Peasantry*, 85.

37. AGEY, PE, Gobernación, caja 16, vol. 3, exp. 29, "Expediente promovido por Pedro Euán, vecino de Muna, contra el juez de paz de dicho pueblo, por abuso de autoridad, para evitar su matrimonio con Tomasa Poot," 1831.

38. AGEY, PE, Gobernación, caja 21, vol. 12, exp. 10, "Representación de Marcelo Uc y otros vecinos de Ebtún querellándose contra el alcalde auxiliar de dicho pueblo por cometer al cobrar las contribuciones civiles y eclesiásticas," 1840.

39. AGEY, PE, Gobernación, caja 17, vol. 4, exp. 21, "Información producida contra el alcalde de Calkiní, en relación a una queja del cacique del pueblo de San Antonio Sahcabchén," 1832.

40. AGEY, PE, Justicia, caja 23, vol. 1, exp. 21, "Información promovido por los indios de Pich, partido de Beneficios Altos, contra Propocio Cocom, por excesos en su función de cacique de dicho pueblo," 1827.

41. AGEY, PE, Gobernación, caja 18, vol. 6, exp. 18, "Información promovida por la república de indios de Dzitbalché, pueblo del partido de Hecelchakan, quienes acusan a Tomás Hernández, alcalde conciliador y cura Fray José León Marin por malos tratos y haber separado sin delito al cacique que tenían," 1832.

42. AGEY, Justicia, Penal, vol. 10, exp. 28, "Sumaria instruida contra Juan Bautista Canul, cacique de Tepich, por exigir dinero a los indígenas a cambio de sus contribuciones," 1833.

43. AGEY, PE, Justicia, caja 24, vol. 2, exp. 7, "Información promovida por Antonio Gutiérrez, subdelegado del partido de Tihosuco, contra el cacique de la república de indígenas de Tahdziú, por abandono de su empleo," 1829; AGEY, PE, Justicia, caja 24, vol. 2, exp. 12, "Información promovido por Baltazar Canché,

contra el cacique de la república de indios de Telá, partido de Tihosuco, por conducta escandalosa, dando lugar a su destitución," 1829.

44. AGEY, PE, Gobernación, caja 16, vol. 2, exp. 4, "Copiador del decretos del año 1829 (incompleto)," 1829.

45. Rugeley, *Yucatán's Maya Peasantry*, 62.

46. AGEY, PE, Gobernación, caja 16, vol. 2, exp. 4, 1829.

47. Of course, in most cases this did not benefit the servants, who simply became more indebted to the hacendados. See Rugeley, *Yucatán's Maya Peasantry*, 75.

48. A *sitio* is a small (usually measuring a square league) privately owned piece of land used for raising bees and livestock. The owner of a sitio was most often Maya. Alexander, *Yaxcabá*, 167.

49. Quoted in Caplan, *Indigenous Citizens*, 108.

50. AGEY, PE, Justicia, Abuso de Autoridad, caja 24, vol. 2, exp. 2, "Juicio promovido por Manuel Antonio Castellanos, vecino de Acanceh, contra Francisco Manrique, alcalde concilador de Teabo, por abuso de autoridad," 1828.

51. Jeffrey Brannon and Gilbert Joseph, eds., *Land, Labor, and Capital in Modern Yucatán: Essays in Regional History and Political Economy* (Tuscaloosa: University of Alabama Press, 2002), 79.

52. It is also possible that this was a case of collusion between the hacendado and the cacique. According to Güémez Pineda, in many cases it was indebted servants who fled haciendas and became "vagrants." To mitigate this situation, authorities of pueblos were often used by hacendados to control vagrancy. See José Arturo Güémez Pineda, "Everyday Forms of Maya Rustling," in Brannon and Joseph, *Land, Labor, and Capital*, 30.

53. AGEY, Justicia, Civil, vol. 27, exp. 22, "Litigio promovido por miembros de la república de indios del pueblo de Nohcacab respecto a un pozo que aparentemente forma parte de la propiedad de Miguel Quijano," 1841.

54. AGEY, PE, Gobernación, caja 17, vol. 4, exp. 18, "Expediente promovido por el C. Pablo José Pérez, contra el C. Benito Fuentes, alcalde conciliador del pueblo de Cantamayec, partido de Sotuta, por abusos de autoridad," 1832.

55. AGEY, PE, Justicia, caja 24, vol. 3, exp. 17, "Expediente promovido por Juan Antonio Keb y otro vecinos del pueblo de Nohcacab, contra Luciano Negro alcalde de dicho pueblo por atropellos en sus personas," 1832.

56. AGEY, PE, Gobernación, caja 17, vol. 4, exp. 2, "Representación de la república de indígenas del pueblo de Tecoh, denunciando el rigor con que les cobran las contribuciones," 1832.

57. AGEY, PE, Gobernación, caja 18, vol. 6, exp. 31, "Representación de varios vecinos de Kaua, partido de Valladolid, contra el alcalde el C. José Novelo, por malos tratos en sus personas y intereses," 1835.

58. AGEY, PE, Justicia, Penal, vol. 23, exp. 26, "Causa seguida por el Juez de primera instancia de Valladolid, a José Sabino Pat y Socios, vecinos de Dzitnup, por tumultuarios," 1841.

59. AGEY, PE, Correspondencia Oficial, caja 9, vol. 5, exp. 3, "Corespondencia del jefe político de Valladolid con el gobernador del este departamento," 1836.

60. AGEY, PE, caja 25, vol. 4, exp. 15, "Diligencias promovida a pedimento de Andrés Canché depuesto cacique por acusaciones que hace el subdelegado de Valladolid," 1837.

61. AGEY, PE, Justicia, caja 24, vol. 2, exp. 12, "Información promovido por Baltazar Canché, contra el cacique de la república de Indios de Telá, partido de Tihosuco, por conducta escandalosa, dando lugar a su destitución," 1829.

62. AGEY, PE, Justicia, caja 24, vol. 2, exp. 7, "Información promovida por Antonio Gutiérrez, subdelegado del partido de Tihosuco, contra el cacique de la república de indígenas de Tahdziú, por abandono de su empleo," 1829.

63. AGEY, PE, Gobernación, caja 16, vol. 2, exp. 47, "Representación de los alcaldes, regidores y vecinos del pueblo indígena de Chichanhá, denunciando el proceder despotico de su cacique," 1831.

64. For instance, in the case of the cacique of San Antonio Sahcabchén: AGEY, PE, Gobernación, caja 17, vol. 4, exp. 21, "Información producida contra el alcalde de Calkiní, en relación a una queja del cacique del pueblo de San Antonio Sahcabchén," 1832.

65. AGEY, PE, Gobernación, caja 17, vol. 4, exp. 14, "Representacion de la republica de indios del pueblo de Sambula, contra el subdelegado del partido, por exigirles trabajos en las Salinas," 1832.

66. AGEY, PE, Gobernación, caja 44, vol. 1, exp. 1, "Diligencias promovidas por Don Mauricio May, cacique suspenso del pueblo de Xoquen, partido de Valladolid, contra Don Santiago de la Cruz Pérez alcalde auxiliar de dicho pueblo por abusos de autoridad," 1841.

67. AGN, Bienes Nacionales, vol 9, exp. 22, 1839, reprinted in Pedro Bracamonte y Sosa, *La memoria enclaustrada: historia indígena de Yucatán, 1750–1915* (Mexico, D.F: CIESAS, 1994), 197.

68. AGEY, PE, Gobernación, caja 44, vol. 1, exp. 1, 1841.

69. AGEY, Justicia, Penal, vol. 20, exp. 2, "Averiguacion promovida por los indígenas Jacinto y Cecilio Pat, vecinos de Tihosuco, contra Perfecto Bolis, juez del mismo pueblo, por abuso de autoridad," 1838–39.

3. For God, Glory, and Taxes

1. AGEY, PE, caja 25, vol. 4, exp. 15, "Diligencias promovida a pedimento de Andrés Canché depuesto cacique por acusaciones que hace el subdelegado de Valladolid," 1837.

2. Ibid.

3. AGEY, PE, Justicia, Penal, vol. 19, exp. 48, "Causa instruida a Eusebio May cacique que fue de Nohcacab y Victoriano Chan de la misma ciudad, para la enajenación de sus bienes embargadas por cubrir el fraude que cometieron en perjuicio de la hacienda publica," 1839.

4. AGEY, PE, Justicia, Penal, vol. 29, exp. 21, "Causa instruida contra Patricio Poot cacique de Ebtún y otras personas de la misma vecindad, por haber defraudado a la hacienda publica de dicho pueblo," 1842.

5. Quoted in Caplan, *Indigenous Citizens*, 107.

6. AGEY, PE, Gobernación, caja 16, vol. 3, exp. 47, "Los alcaldes y justicias de la republica de indios de Hunucmá proponiendo una terna para designación de su cacique y de los individuos que han ejercer los cargos el proximo año," 1831.

7. Caplan, *Indigenous Citizens*, 137.

8. AGEY, PE, Justicia, caja 23, vol. 1, exp. 12, "Información producida contra Pedro Caamal, cacique del barrio de San Cristóbal, por allanamiento de casas de unos vecinos," 1825.

9. AGEY, Justicia, Penal, vol. 3, exp. 23, "Causa criminal contra Juan de Mata Cocom por incitar a los indígenas de Timucuy a no pagar sus contribuciones," 1825; Melchor Campos García, "Faccionalismo y votaciones en Yucatán, 1824–1832," *Historia Mexicana* 51, no. 1 (2001), 80.

10. AGEY, PE, Gobernación, caja 18, vol. 6, exp. 28, "Representación de la república de indígenas de Seyé, pidiendo prorroga para pagar sus impuestos personales, por la escasez de granos," 1835.

11. Ibid.

12. AGEY, PE, Gobernación, caja 18, vol. 6, exp. 18, "Información promovida por la república de indios de Dzitbalché, pueblo del partido de Hecelchakan, quienes acusan a Tomás Hernández, alcalde conciliador y cura Fray José León Martín por malos tratos y haber separado sin delito al cacique que tenían," 1832.

13. AGEY, PE, Gobernación, caja 15, vol. 1, exp. 29, "Sumaria información contra Lázaro Caamal, cacique de Yaxcabá, por ineptitud in el cobro de contribución personal y auto de destitución del mismo," 1827.

14. AGEY, PE, Empleos, caja 14, vol. 2, exp. 49, "Renuncia de Juan Pablo Caamal cacique de Kancabdzonot, pueblo del curato de Yaxcabá, y designación de Luciano May para dicho empleo," 1829.

15. Quoted in Caplan, *Indigenous Citizens*, 38.

16. AGEY, Colonial, Varios, caja 32, vol. 1, exp. 18, "Indios, representación de Fray Pedro Guzmán, cura de Uayma, sobre la conducta observada por los indios al otorgarles su libertad de la constitución," 1813.

17. AGEY, Colonial, Varios, vol. 1, exp. 16, "Indios, representación del cacique, regidores y justicias del pueblo de Tinum por diferencias con el cura doctrinero Fray Pablo Carrillo por unas contribuciones," 1813.

Created by the Cortes of Cádiz, the Diputaciónes Provinciales were intended to be the medium between the national and the regional or local levels and were charged with the governance and supervision of the provinces. Reflecting the tumultuous events in Spain, these offices in Mexico existed briefly between 1812 and 1814 and then again in 1820–21 (under Spanish rule) and after Mexican independence till 1823. For more on the Diputación Provincial, see Nettie Lee Benson, *The Provincial Deputation in Mexico: Harbinger of Provincial Autonomy, Independence, and Federalism* (Austin: University of Texas Press, 1992).

18. "Sesión 14," Libro Copiador de actas, num. 104, 30 Oct 1820, in María Zuleta, ed., *La diputación provincial de Yucatán: actas de sesiones, 1813–1814, 1820–1821* (Mexico City: Instituto de Investigaciones Dr. José María Luis Mora, 2006), 447.

19. Terry Rugeley, "From Santa Iglesia to Santa Cruz: Yucatecan Popular Religion in Peace and War, 1800–1876," in Edward Terry et al., eds., *Peripheral Visions: Politics, Society and the Challenges of Modernity in Yucatán* (Tuscaloosa: University of Alabama Press, 2010), 190.

20. AGEY, PE, Gobernación, caja 16, vol. 3, exp. 21, "Expediente promovido por los alcaldes y justicias de los ranchos Chac y Kauil, anexos del pueblo de Nohkakab, curato de Ticul en Sierra Alta contra el juez de paz de ese partido por la forma en que les exige el pago de sus tributos," 1831.

21. AGEY, PE, Gobernación, caja 16, vol. 2, exp. 47, "Representación de los alcaldes, regidores y vecinos del pueblo indígena de Chichanhá, denunciando el proceder despótico de su cacique," 1831.

22. AGEY, PE, Justicia, caja 24, vol. 3, exp. 5, "Información por una denuncia del cura de Kopomá, contra el juez de paz de dicho pueblo, por impedir que los vecinos paguen los derechos de una contrata de entierros," 1831.

23. AGEY, PE, Gobernación, caja 16, vol. 2, exp. 55, "Representación del cacique y justicias del pueblo de Baca, subdelegación de la Costa sobre el pago de obvenciones parroquiales," 1831.

24. AGEY, PE, Gobernación, caja 16, vol. 3, exp. 21, "Expediente promovido por los alcaldes y justicias de los ranchos Chac y Kauil, anexos del pueblo de Nohkakab, curato de Ticul en Sierra Alta contra el juez de paz de ese partido por la forma en que les exige el pago de sus tributos," 1831.

25. AGEY, PE, Gobernación, caja 16, vol. 3, exp. 11, "Expediente promovido por el subdelegado del partido de Hunucmá, para que el Pbro. Pedro José Montañez, residente del pueblo de Opichén, desocupe la casa del posito del dicho pueblo," 1831.

26. The importance of education comes through in the Diputación Provincial documents, which address the grants and salaries given to maestros. These documents show that in many cases the maestro was granted more money than an administrative official such as secretary of an ayuntamiento. See "Sesion 1a," 7 May 1814, Arbirtrio de Dzidzantún in Zuleta, *La Diputación Provincial*, 274; "Sesion 6a," 14 June 1814, ibid., 298.

27. Education was to serve the purpose of creating the "new" Mexican citizen. Vázquez de Knauth writes, "Having just achieved independence, it was intended to utilize the school to create a new type of citizen in accordance with the aspirations of the new political order." See Josefina Zoraida Vázquez de Knauth, *Nacionalismo y educación en México* (Mexico City: El Colegio de Mexico, 1970), 2 (my translation).

28. AGEY, PE, Gobernación, caja 16, vol. 3, exp. 34, "Acuerdo de que se reponga a Marcelino Puch, en su empleo de cacique que del barrio de Santiago de Mérida, del que fue suspendido por inodado en una conspiración, por estar comprendido en el decreto de aministía," 1831.

29. Michael Meyer, William Sherman, and Susan Deeds, *The Course of Mexican History* (New York: Oxford University Press, 2010), 328.

30. Terry Rugeley, *Maya Wars: Ethnographic Accounts from Nineteenth-Century Yucatán* (Norman: University of Oklahoma Press, 2001), 9.

31. Don Dumond, *The Machete and the Cross: Campesino Rebellion in Yucatan* (Lincoln: University of Nebraska Press, 1997), 71.

32. "Decreto de 9 de Septiembre de 1840," in Alonso Aznar Pérez, *Colección de leyes, decretos y ordenes: o acuerdos de tendencia general, del poder legislativo del estado libre y soberano de Yucatán*, vol. 1 (Mérida: Imprenta del Editor, 1849), 316; "Articulo 3: las autoridades locales auxiliarán eficazmente el pago del referido impuesto y el de las obvenciones adeudadas," ibid., 317.

33. AGEY, PE, Gobernación, caja 21, vol. 12, exp. 10, "Representación de Marcelo Uc y otros vecinos de Ebtún querellándose contra el alcalde auxiliar de dicho pueblo por cometer al cobrar las contribuciones civiles y eclesiásticas," 1840.

34. Ibid.

35. This can be seen, for instance, in a case in Sotuta where Pedro Pascual Ku and other indígenas complained that their cacique and justicias were still collecting obvenciones from them. AGEY, PE, Gobernación, caja 21, vol. 12, exp. 12, "Expediente promovido por Pedro Pascual Ku y otros vecinos de Cuzamá contra el cacique de dicho pueblo del partido de Sotuta," 1840.

36. For example, AGEY, PE, Gobernación, caja 21, vol. 12, exp. 17, "Representación de los vecinos del rancho Jotoech, partido de Valladolid, por malos tratos que reciben del alcalde de Chemax," 1840.

37. AGEY, Justicia, Civil, vol. 37, exp. 22, "Causa instruida contra la república de indígenas del pueblo de Hopelchen por resistencia al pago de contribuciones," 1845.

38. AGEY, PE, Gobernación, caja 21, vol. 12, exp. 17, 1840.

39. AGEY, PE, Gobernación, caja 21, vol. 12, exp. 10, 1840.

40. AGEY, PE, Gobernación, caja 21, vol. 12, exp. 12, 1840.

41. AGEY, PE, Gobernación, caja 21, vol. 14, exp. 29, "Representación de Pablo José Reyes alcalde de Calkini, calificando de falsedad los hechos que le atribuyeron en las elecciones parroquiales de dicha villa," 1840.

42. AGEY, PE, Gobernación, caja 21, vol. 14, exp. 13, "Representación de Joseph Sotero Brito, cura interino de la parroquia de Peto, acusando al alcalde Don Felipe Rosado de manda que no paguen los derechos de estola establecidas para la parroquia," 1840. Felipe Rosado would become an important figure in the Caste War and would lead the Peto battalion of the Yucatecan militia in 1848. See Dumond, *Machete and the Cross*, 104.

43. AGEY, PE, Gobernación, caja 21, vol. 13, exp. 15, "Información promovida por Don Clemente Uc, cacique de la república de indígenas de Dzibalchen, para probar que reúne las condiciones necesarias para continuar ejerciendo dicho cargo," 1840.

44. AGEY, PE, Gobernación, caja 21, vol. 12, exp. 27, "Destitución de Don Pablo Cauich, cacique de Tixkokob, consecuencia de la sumaria instruida por el alcalde de dicho pueblo, comprobando su mala conducta," 1840.

45. AGEY, PE, Justicia, Penal, vol. 10, exp. 28, July 1833.

4. War and the Cacique

Epigraph. "Through Blood and Fire: Cecilio Chi's Letter to John Fancourt," in Rugeley, *Maya Wars*, 53–54.

1. "Decreto de 2 de Enero de 1850," in Aznar Pérez, *Colección de leyes*, vol. 3, 308.

2. AGEY, PE, Empleos, caja 105, vol. 55, exp. 34, "Jefe político de Espita se dirige al secretario general de gobierno recomendando al indigena Andrés Canché, para cacique de Cenotillo," 1852.

3. The Caste War began in 1847 and then intensified until 1852–53, when the rebels were pushed south. Thereafter the fighting shifted to Chan Santa Cruz in what is now the state of Quintana Roo. The scholarly consensus is that the Caste War continued till the turn of the twentieth century.

4. By using examples of nonrebel caciques, this chapter complements Caste War studies such as Terry Rugeley's path-breaking *Yucatan's Maya Peasantry*, which among other things examines the historical processes that led to caciques providing leadership to the rebels.

5. Wolfgang Gabbert, *Becoming Maya: Ethnicity and Social Inequality in Yucatán since 1500* (Tucson: University of Arizona Press, 2004), 63.

6. For a discussion of the meanings associated with the term "vecino," see Tamar Herzog, *Defining Nations: Immigrants and Citizens in Early Modern Spain and Spanish America* (New Haven: Yale University Press, 2011), chaps 2–3.

7. Rugeley, *Maya Wars*, 10–11, 52.

8. Gabbert, *Becoming Maya*, 49, 64, 69.

9. "Ley de 27 de Agosto de 1847," in Aznar Pérez, *Colección de leyes*, vol. 3, 150–51.

10. García, *Las constituciones historicas*, 429.

11. Aznar Pérez, *Colección de leyes*, vol. 3, 146.

12. That the 1847 decree was meant as a punitive measure can be inferred from the language of the decree itself. Dumond makes a similar point in *Machete and the Cross*, 96–100.

13. Arturo Güémez Pineda, "Municipalización y guerra de castas: testimonios de la restricción a la libertad civil maya en Yucatán, 1847–1869," in Melchor Campos García, *Republicanismos emergentes: continuidades y rupturas en Yucatán y Puebla, 1786–1869* (Mérida: Universidad Autónoma de Yucatán, 2010). For effects of municipalization in the pre–Caste War period, see Arturo Güémez Pineda, *Mayas,*

gobierno y tierras frente a la acometida liberal en Yucatán, 1812–1847 (Mérida: Universidad Autónoma de Yucatán, 2005).

14. Aznar Pérez, *Colección de leyes*, vol. 3, 150.

15. "Decreto de 14 de Enero de 1848," in ibid., 174.

16. Nelson Reed, *The Caste War of Yucatán* (Stanford, Calif.: Stanford University Press, 2001), 186.

17. AGEY, PE, Correspondencia Oficial, caja 94, vol. 44, exp. 21, "Comunicados de Evencio Osorno y Fermin de Irabien al gobernador acerca de: manifestaciones de fincas y parajes de indios; proposiciones en terna para cacique de Chichimila etc.," 1860.

18. AGEY, PE, Ayuntamientos, Jefatura Politica de Motul, caja 62, vol. 12, exp. 115, "José Cirerol comunica al gobernador el informe de la junta municipal de Tixkokob de la solicitud del cacique de la república de indígenas para que se les exceptue del servicio de faginas," 1862.

19. Rugeley, *Rebellion Now and Forever*, 82; Rugeley, *Maya Wars*, 141.

20. "Decreto de 14 de Enero de 1848," in Aznar Pérez, *Colección de leyes*, vol. 3, 173.

21. Dumond, *Machete and the Cross*, 119.

22. AGEY, PE, Gobernación, caja 124, vol. 74, exp. 18, "Bernardino Tzakum, cacique de la república de indígenas de Yaxcabá, solicita al gobernador le admita su renuncia de dicho encargo," 1857.

23. AGEY, PE, Gobernación, caja 122, vol. 72, exp. 96, "Solicitud de Nicolás Uh al gobernador para renunciar al cargo de cacique de la república de indígenas del pueblo de Oxkutzcab," 1856.

24. AGEY, PE, Gobernación, caja 124, vol. 74, exp. 3, "Manuel Couoh cacique de la república de indígenas de Izamal, presenta renuncia al gobernador," 1857.

25. AGEY, PE, Correspondencia Oficial, caja 98, vol. 48, exp. 78, "Comunicaciones de José D. Espinosa y Rios al gobernador acerca de: abono del importe de boletas para elecciones; acusa de recibo de ejemplares de decreto; propuesta para cacique de la república de indígenas a Manuel Couoh; etc.," 1862.

26. AGEY, PE, Correspondencia Oficial, caja 87, vol. 37, exp. 25, "Pedro Rubio informa al gobernador que el cacique del suburbio de Santa Ana no realiza el cobro de contribución de los de su raza y solicita su destitución," 1856.

27. AGEY, PE, Correspondencia Oficial, caja 96, vol. 46, exp. 13, "Comunicaciones de Manuel Pardio y otros al gobernador acerca de: no ocurre novedad; nombramiento de cacique al indigena Francisco Mena; envio del acta de examen de alumnos de primeras letras; etc.," 1862.

28. AGEY, Justicia, Penal, vol. 113, exp. 4, "Diligencias practicadas contra el juez de paz de Suma, Eusebio Gallegos y quejas del cacique José María Pech," 1862.

29. AGEY, PE, Correspondencia Oficial, caja 96, vol. 46, exp. 6, "Comunicados de José D. Sosa al gobernador acerca de: aclaracion de unos rumores infundados

de la creación de cuerpos de linea; separación del alcalde primero de la carcel; cambio del cacique de Caucel etc.," 1861.

30. The source of the documents concerning the Angelino Uicab case—including the petitions from Uicab and other indígenas to the governor and jefe político as well as correspondence of the jefe político and the jueces of Teya, Cansahcab, Izamal, the letter of Buenaventura Castillo, and the testimonies of the indígenas—is a single file: AGEY, Justicia, Penal, Abuso de Autoridad, vol. 58, exp. 43 "Expediente formado con motivo de la mala conducta de Angelino Uicab cacique del pueblo de Teya, partido de Motul," 1850–51. Unless otherwise noted, all evidence, quotations, and the like for the Teya case come from this file.

31. AGEY, PE, Correspondencia Oficial, caja 76, vol. 26, exp. 53, "Comunicaciones de Andrés de Zepeda al secretario general de gobierno referente a la toma de dzilam por los rebeldes; asi como haber caído Tepakan y Teya; a haberse recuperado zilam por abandonar los rebeldes, etc," 1848.

32. Dumond, *Machete and the Cross*, 179. After 1848, the tide of war turned against the Maya rebels and they began to be pushed to the east. In 1850, Maya rebel leaders established their new base at a cenote called Chan Santa Cruz (Little Holy Cross). Near the cenote was a mahogany tree on which was found carved an image of the cross. A cult soon emerged around this cross, which "spoke" to the Maya through a ventriloquist. Later the cross would "speak" through select scribes or prophets, and sometimes it would multiply itself so that several crosses were found in different villages. The rebel followers of the cross were known as the Cruzob, and they remained the main Maya opponents to the Yucatecan government in the nineteenth century. Matthew Restall, *2012 and the End of the World: The Western Roots of the Maya Apocalypse* (Lanham, Md.: Rowman and Littlefield, 2011), 109; Terry Rugeley *Of Wonders and Wise Men: Religion and Popular Culture in Southeast Mexico, 1800–1876* (Austin: University of Texas Press, 2001), 111.

33. Documents from 1852 and 1853 explicitly state that Gregorio Lara was juez segundo. In addition, correspondence from Andrés de Zepeda to the governor suggests that jueces of the partido of Motul from the previous years were reelected in 1852. See AGEY, PE, Correspondencia Oficial, caja 80, vol. 30, exp. 7, 3 January to 27 December 1852. This again suggests that the juez segundo of 1852, Gregorio Lara, had also served in the preceding year, during the time of the case of Angelino Uicab. Taking all this into consideration, it is reasonable to assume that Gregorio Lara functioned as the juez segundo during 1851.

34. AGEY, Justicia, Penal, vol. 45, exp. 48, "Causa instruida contra D. Cornelio Souza y D. Macedonio Dzul, cacique de Peto, por reunión tumultuaria y asonada," 1845.

35. AGEY, Justicia, Penal, vol. 26, exp. 30, "Causa instruida contra José Luis Silviera, alcalde del pueblo de Yaxkukul, por abuso de autoridad con motivo del arresto arbitrario del cacique de la república de indígenas del mismo pueblo," 1842.

36. AGEY, PE, Justicia, caja 144, vol. 94, exp. 70, "Traducción de la comunicación interceptada a Luis se dirigida al cacique de Kancabdzonot Francisco Camal invitandolo a levantarse en armas firmada por Cecilio Chí, Jacinto Pat y otros," 1847.

37. Rugeley, *Yucatán's Maya Peasantry*, 82; José Mauricio Dzul Sanchez, "José Matias Quintana y las organizaciones precursoras del movimiento liberal yucateco 1812–1823," *Archivo General del Estado de Yucatán*, www.archivogeneral.yucatan.gob.mx/Bicentenario/JMQ%20Organizacion%20precursoras%20yucatecas.htm (accessed 19 January 2016).

38. Rugeley, *Rebellion Now and Forever*, 118.

39. AGEY, PE, Correspondencia Oficial, caja 76, vol. 26, exp. 81, "Andrés de Zepeda se dirige al secretario general de gobierno comunicándole haber remitido unas actas; dificultad para reunir el maíz para socorro de los soldados en campaña; aprehensión de sublevados etc.," 1848.

40. AGEY, PE, Partidos, libro 28, "Correspondencia del Gobernador Don Miguel Barbachano con las autoridades de los departamentos de Izamal y Valladolid," 1851.

41. "Table showing the parish of Teya and its auxiliary Tepakam, and the number of souls," 1 May 1821, in Dumond and Dumond, *Demography and Parish Affairs*, 251.

42. AGEY, Justicia, Penal, Abuso de Autoridad, vol. 63, exp. 23, "Diligencias practicada contra el juez segundo de paz de Teya D. Gregorio Lara por abusos de autoridad," 1852.

43. AGEY, PE, Justicia, caja 145, vol. 95, exp. 56, "El secretario general de gobierno turna al juez de 1a instancia de Izamal la queja de José Gregorio Lara contra los procedimientos del juez de paz de Teya y del jefe político de Motul," 1853.

44. Ibid.; AGEY, PE, Correspondencia Oficial, caja 82, vol. 32, exp. 20, "Andrés De Zepeda informa al secretario general de gobierno sobre amancebamiento que lleva Gregorio Lara, juez de paz de Teya con Isabel Meña," 1853.

45. AGEY, PE, Milicia, caja 164, vol. 114, exp. 48, "El comandante de la división envía al comandante de Mérida la correspondencia tomada a los indios de Cenotillo," 1848.

46. Dumond, *Machete and the Cross*, 145.

47. AGEY, PE, caja 80, vol. 30, exp. 1, "Correspondencia de jefe político de Espita al secretario general," 1852.

48. AGEY, PE, Gobernación, caja 120, vol. 70, exp. 124, "Marco Antonio Peniche comunica al gobernador la queja del Juez de paz y del cura de Cenotillo contra el cacique Andrés Canché," 1855.

49. AGEY, PE, Justicia, Penal, caja 144, vol. 94, exp. 50, "Joaquin Cetina y Pablo Lujan informan al secretario general de gobierno de los asesinatos perpetrados por Don Pastor Gamboa del cacique, alcalde y escribano de la republica de indigenas," 1847.

50. AGEY, PE, Gobernación, caja 120, vol. 70, exp. 124.

51. AGEY, PE, Administración, caja 52, vol. 2, exp. 4, "German Che cacique de la Republica de Indios de Espita solicita al gobernador, su renuncia por motivos de salud," 1847.

52. AGEY, PE, Gobernacion; caja 50, vol. 2, exp. 42, "El gobernador concediendo a Anselmo Kenel, cacique de Xul, partido de Tekax, la renuncia que solicita por motivos de salud," 1842.

53. AGEY, PE, Empleos, caja 105, vol. 55, exp. 21, "Propuesta enviada al secretario general del gobierno por el Juez de paz de Nunkini y Cura de Becal para ocupar el cargo por fallecimiento del cacique Apolonio Trejo y José Jacinto Colli," 1852.

54. AGEY, PE, Gobernación, caja 19, vol. 9, exp. 24, "Designación de Luciano Mis, para cacique del pueblo de Dzibalché del partido de Hecelchakán, por renuncia del que tenía ese empleo," 1837.

55. "Ley de 5 de Abril de 1841," in Aznar Pérez, *Colección de leyes*, vol. 2, 116.

56. "Decreto de 16 Noviembre de 1843," in ibid., 285.

57. Rugeley, *Yucatán's Maya Peasantry*, 123–25, quote 124.

58. Pedro Bracamonte y Sosa, *Amos y sirvientes: las haciendas de Yucatán, 1789–1860* (Mérida: Universidad Autónoma de Yucatán, 1993), 108.

59. Paul Eiss, *In the Name of El Pueblo: Place, Community, and the Politics of History in Yucatán* (Durham, N.C.: Duke University Press, 2010), 40.

60. Caplan, *Indigenous Citizens*, 209.

61. "Decreto of 23 Noviembre 1844," in Aznar Pérez, *Colección de leyes*, vol. 2, 369.

62. "Decreto de 3 de Julio 1860," in Eligio Ancona, *Colección de leyes, decretos, ordenes y demás disposiciones de tendencia general: expedidas por el poder legislativo del estado de Yucatan* (Mérida: Imp. de El Eco del Comercio, 1882–89), 92.

63. Nevertheless, it appears that these laws did not really succeed in the long run. By 1869 only 117,000 head of cattle were to be found in Yucatán. See Douglas Richmond, *Conflict and Carnage in Yucatán: Liberals, the Second Empire, and Maya Revolutionaries, 1855–1876* (Tuscaloosa: University of Alabama Press, 2015), 82.

64. AGEY, PE, Correspondencia Oficial, caja 221, vol. 171, exp. 17, "Buenaventura Cabrera comandante de la guardia nacional y Andrés Canché cacique de indígenas en representación de sus subordinados solicitan al gobernador la derogación del decreto de 3 de Julio de 1860 sobre poblamiento de ganado por afectar a sus interés," 1863.

65. Ibid.

66. Rugeley, *Rebellion Now and Forever*, 204.

67. AGEY, PE, Justicia, caja 145, vol. 95, exp. 14, "Andrés de Zepeda envia al secretario general del gobierno las diligencias practicadas por la queja del cacique de la república de indígenas de Yaxkukul contra el juez de paz 2° Juan Bautista Monforte," 1851; AGEY, PE, Correspondencia Oficial, caja 78, vol. 28, exp. 65, "Andrés de Zepeda comunica al secretario general de gobierno la aperture de escuela, designación de jueces de paz; terna de caciques de la república de indígenas; y etc.," 1851.

68. AGEY, PE, Correspondencia Oficial, caja 84, vol. 34, exp. 27, "Andrés de Zepeda se dirige al secretario general de gobierno en referencia al reemplazo de Juan Pascual Poot, cacique de Yaxkukul en forma aparentemente injustificada," 1854.

69. AGEY, PE, Gobernación, caja 119, vol. 69, exp. 79, "Pablo Silveira comunica al secretario general de gobierno el informe por el que Juan Pascual Poot fue despojado del cargo de cacique de la república de indios," 1854; AGEY, PE, Correspondencia Oficial, caja 84, vol. 34, exp. 24, "Comunicados de Pablo Silbeira al secretario general de gobierno acerca del nombramiento del cacique de la república de indios de Yaxkukul," 1854.

5. "Your Majesty Loves the Indians"

1. Frederic Hall, *Invasion of Mexico by the French; And the Reign of Maximilian I; with a Sketch of the Empress Carlota* (New York: James Miller, 1868), 47, 49.

2. Larson, *Trials of Nation Making*, 133.

3. Meyer et al., *Course of Mexican History*, 394–95; Rugeley, *Rebellion Now and Forever*, 225.

4. Cutter, *Protector de Indios*, 9.

5. Rugeley, *Maya Wars*, 148.

6. For a recent analysis of the impact of haciendas in the 1880s and after, see Piedad Peniche Rivero, *La historia secreta de la hacienda henequenera de Yucatán: deudas, migración y resistencia maya, 1879–1915* (Mérida: Instituto de Cultura de Yucatán, 2010). Allen Wells's and Gil Joseph's works still remain the classics: Allen Wells, *Yucatan's Gilded Age: Haciendas, Henequen, and International Harvester, 1860–1915* (Albuquerque: University of New Mexico Press, 1985); Allen Wells and Gil Joseph, *Summer of Discontent, Seasons of Upheaval: Elite Politics and Rural Insurgency in Yucatán, 1876–1915* (Stanford, Calif.: Stanford University Press, 1996).

7. Bracamonte y Sosa, *La memoria enclaustrada*, fig. 9, 148.

8. According to Friedrich Katz, in nineteenth- and twentieth-century Mexico, the term "peon" was used to designate laborers, either in agriculture or in mining. Resident peons (also known as *peones acasillados*) lived permanently on their masters' haciendas. The institution of peonage became increasingly onerous in the early nineteenth century, and in 1843 a law passed in Yucatán "made it illegal to hire laborers who had left an hacienda without paying their debts and required local authorities to return indebted peons to their haciendas." Friedrich Katz, "Labor Conditions on Haciendas in Porfirian Mexico: Some Trends and Tendencies," *Hispanic American Historical Review* 54, no. 1, 1974, 2–4, quote 8.

9. Dumond and Dumond, *Demographic and Parish Affairs*, 126.

10. AGEY, Justicia, Civil, Deudas, vol. 108, exp. 11, "Juicio promovido por el apoderado de Juan José Mendez contra el indigena Tus y sus dos hijos y Manuel Bacab para que vuelvan a su servicio," 1863.

11. CAIHY, "Informe de los trabajos realizados durante la visita del Abogado Defensor de Indios a los pueblos del oriente," XLVIII -1865 -1/4 -007, 1865. After a month-long tour of the villages in eastern Yucatán in January 1865, Molina sent an unusually detailed report of his trip to the comisario imperial, Salazar Ilarregui. This document is one of the most important sources for our understanding of the kinds of cases the defensor encountered and the obstacles he faced in attempting reform.

12. For example, during his journey through pueblos in Yucatán in 1865, Molina came across indigenous people such as Julian Poc and José Canul, who sought the defensor's help in acquiring the carta cuenta from their masters. See CAIHY, "Informe de los trabajos," 1865.

13. AGEY, Justicia, Civil, Deudas, vol. 123, exp. 32, "Juicio por el Defensor Auxiliar de naturales en representación del Gervacio Xiu contra su amo Estanislao Cámara para que se libre su carta cuenta," 1865.

14. AGEY, Justicia, Penal, Injurias, vol. 126, exp. 43, "Queja de Eleuterio Chalé por medio del defensor de indios contra su amo Don Gumesindo Ruiz por injuria real," 1864.

15. AGEY, Justicia, Civil, Oficios, vol. 117, exp. 12, "Demanda del apoderado de Joaquín B. Vargas contra los indígenas Francisco Koyoc, Juan Ventura Chan y Juan Cetz por separarse del servicio de la hacienda Balche," 1865.

16. AGEY, Justicia, Civil, Deudas, vol. 123, exp. 10, "Juicio de conciliación del defensor auxiliar de naturales en representación del indigena Aniceto Chim demandando a Don Joaquín B. Vargas," 1865.

17. CAIHY, "Informe de los trabajos," 1865; AGEY, Justicia, Civil, Deudas, vol. 121, exp. 15, "Juicio por el agente auxiliar de la defensor de naturales en representación del indígena Juan Crisóstomo Chablé contra José de los Angeles Ortega por deuda," 1865.

18. CAIHY, "Informe de los trabajos," 1865.

19. This practice seems to have continued throughout the nineteenth century. Gil Joseph writes that children of hacienda peons were often taken to the planters' homes in Mérida to work as domestic servants. See Wells and Joseph, *Summer of Discontent*, 163.

20. CAIHY, "Informe de los trabajos," 1865.

21. AGEY, Justicia, Civil, vol. 116, exp. 40, "Diligencias del defensor de naturales representando al menor Tiburcio Yam, por nombramiento del curador," 1865.

22. Wells, *Yucatán's Gilded Age*, 154.

23. Patch, *Maya and Spaniard in Yucatan*, 151; Bracamonte y Sosa, *Amos y Sirvientes*, 123.

24. AGEY, Justicia, Civil, vol. 117, exp. 34, "Instancia del defensor de naturales en representación de Carmen Ek para que Josefa Mesa le entregue a su hija menor Lugarda Baas," 1865.

25. AGEY, Justicia, Civil, vol. 116, exp. 42, "Diligencias por el defensor de naturales en representación de Manuela Balam para que Doña Micaela Zetina entregue una hija suya que indebidamente tiene en su poder," 1865.

26. AGEY, Justicia, Civil, vol. 127, exp. 18, "Diligencias por el defensor de naturales en representación de Manuela Balam para que Doña Micaela Zetina le entregue una hija suya," 1866.

27. AGEY, Justicia, Civil, Custodia de hijos, vol. 128, exp. 13, "Instancia del Defensor de Indios a favor de Andrea Ceh demandando la devolución de un hijo suyo que tenia en su poder su esposo José María Zakol," 1866.

28. CAIHY, "Informe de los trabajos," 1865.

29. Ibid.

30. On 2 August 1865, for instance, Molina resolved the case brought to him by the sons of Matías Poot for selling the livestock they had inherited. AGEY, Justicia, Civil, vol. 121, exp. 4, "Diligencias por el abogado defensor de naturales Lic. Don José D. Molina en representación de los herederos de Matias Poot para el remate de 3 semovientes de sus bienes," 1865.

31. AGEY, Justicia, Civil, vol. 119, exp. 16, "Juicio promovido por el abogado defensor de naturales en representación de Lázaro Ek contra Doña María Herrera para que levante la albarrada contigua," 1865.

32. AGEY, Justicia, Civil, vol. 123, exp. 21, "Diligencias de mensura de los sitios Copo y Chan Pich de varios indígenas del pueblo de Chicxulub," 1865.

33. Rugeley, *Rebellion Now and Forever*, 204–5.

34. AGEY, Justicia, Civil, vol. 114, exp. 35, "Diligencias promovida por el defensor de indígenas para que se entregue a María Francisca Baas su hija Juliana Can," 1864.

35. AGEY, Justicia, Penal, Abuso de Autoridad, vol. 129, exp. 8, "Diligencias promovida por el defensor de indios contra el juez de paz de Yaxkukul," 1865.

36. CAIHY, "Informe de los trabajos," 1865.

37. AGEY, Justicia, Civil, vol. 116, exp. 36, "Diligencias promovidas por el defensor de Pablo Pech para que el juez de paz segundo de Mérida le entregue copia certificada de un acta de juicio," 1865.

38. AGEY, Justicia, Civil, vol. 122, exp. 16, "Juicio verbal por el defensor de los naturales en representación de Estanislao y Ambrosio Tec contra Don Andrés Urcelay para sus cartas cuentas," 1865.

39. CAIHY, "Informe de los trabajos," 1865.

40. Ibid.

41. Ibid.

42. Quoted in Rugeley, *Maya Wars*, 150.

43. Rugeley, *Rebellion*, 227; Wells, *Yucatán's Gilded Age*, 61.

44. I borrow the phrase from Mark Thurner, *From Two Republics to One Divided: Contradictions of Postcolonial Nation Making in Andean Peru* (Durham, N.C.: Duke University Press, 1997).

6. Of Promises and Dilemmas

1. AGEY, PE, Comisaria Imperial, caja 228, vol. 178, exp. 85, "Comunicado de Andrés Canché al prefecto superior político del departamento acerca de su renuncia como cacique de la republica de indígenas del pueblo de Cenotillo," 1864.

2. Ibid.

3. Quoted in Joan Haslip, *The Crown of Mexico: Maximilian and His Empress Carlota* (New York: Holt, Rinehart and Winston, 1971), 340.

4. Rugeley, *Rebellion Now and Forever*, 203.

5. Ibid., 251.

6. AGEY, PE, Ayuntamientos, caja 226, vol. 176, exp. 94, "José Santiago Piste, Laureano Pech, Sixto Koh y José Irineo Ek solicitan al prefecto superior político los exceptue de sus cargos en la república de indígenas de Kantunil, Temax e Izamal," 1864.

7. AGEY, PE, Ayuntamientos, caja 222, vol. 172, exp. 66, "Romualdo Abad solicita al gobernador lo exceptue del servicio en la república de indígenas de Izamal," 1864.

8. AGEY, PE, Ayuntamientos, caja 223, vol. 173, exp. 15, "Marcelino Mex solicita al gobernador lo exhonere de ser integrante de la republica de indígenas de Acanceh," 1864.

9. AGEY, PE, Ayuntamientos, caja 226, vol. 176, exp. 94, 1864.

10. Ibid.

11. AGEY, PE, Ayuntamientos, caja 232, vol. 182, exp. 13, "Antonino Bolio solicita al prefecto superior político exceptue a su sirviente José Maria Cua del destino de regidor de la republica de indígenas de Santa Ana por las razones que expone," 1865.

12. Rugeley, *Rebellion Now and Forever*, 226.

13. AGEY, PE, Correspondencia Oficial, caja 235, vol. 185, exp. 56, "Comunicado de Antonio Barrera al prefecto del departamento acerca de: nombramiento provisional del cacique de indígenas de Ticul," 1865.

14. AGEY, PE, Comisaría Municipal, caja 226, vol. 176, exp. 87, "Comunicado de Ignacio Cetzal al prefecto superior político del departamento acerca de su renuncia como cacique de la república de indígenas de Espita," 1864.

15. AGEY, PE, Correspondencia Oficial, caja 225, vol. 175, exp. 80, "Comunicado de Juan G. Contreras al prefecto político del departamento acerca de: solicitud de los jueces de paz de Tixkokob para cambiar al cacique José María Poot del pueblo de Euán por sus continuos escándalos," 1864.

16. AGEY, PE, Ayuntamientos, caja 232, vol. 182, exp. 6, "José María Nauat y Anselmo Cocom solicitan al prefecto superior sean repuestos en sus empleos de cacique y teniente de la república de indígenas de Sitpach por las razones que exponen," 1865.

17. AGEY, PE, Ayuntamientos, caja 227, vol. 177, exp. 85, "Anselmo Dzul cacique de la república de indios de Tizimín comunica al prefecto superior del departamento aclarando una declaración que hizo sobre la actuación del subprefecto de Tizimín," 1864.

18. AGEY, PE, Tierras, caja 224, vol. 174, exp. 59, "Teodosio Canto, juez de paz primero y Ambrosio May, cacique de la república de indios solicitan al gobernador el deslinde de ejidos de Cansahcab," 1864.

19. AGEY, PE, Gobernación, caja 224, vol. 174, exp. 63, "Queja de los vecinos de Timucuy al gobernador en contra de su cacique Ignacio Canul por los abusos y atropellos de que los hace victimas," 1864.

20. AGEY, PE, Comisaria Municipal, caja 227, vol. 177, exp. 3, "Los indígenas de la república de Espita solicitan al prefecto superior político se destituya a su cacique por los abusos que comete contra ellos," 1864.

21. AGEY, PE, Correspondencia Oficial, caja 96, vol. 46, exp. 43, "Comunicación de Quintin Pastor al gobernador acerca de: la queja de los jueces de paz de Cacalchén contra el actual cacique Juan J. Xool y propuestas para dicho cargo," 1861.

22. AGEY, PE, Correspondencia Oficial, caja 98, vol. 48, exp. 1, "P. Rosado y Mariano Osorio comunica al gobernador acerca de: propuesta para cacique de Calotmul a Manuel Che," 1862.

23. See, for instance, AGEY, Justicia, Civil, vol. 108, exp. 11, "Juicio promovido por el apoderado de Juan José Mendez contra el indigena Tus y sus dos hijos y Manuel Bacab para que vuelvan a su servicio," 1863.

24. The cacique of Nohcacab, for instance, represented his community and defended the property of the *común* (commons) against landlord Miguel Quijano in 1841. AGEY, Justicia, Civil, vol. 27, exp. 22, "Litigio promovido por miembros de la república de indios por pueblo de Nohcacab respecto a un pozo que aparentemente forma parte de la propiedad de Miguel Quijano," 1841. Similarly in Hunucmá in 1856–57, the cacique Pascual Chac was involved in an extended case against hacendado Juana Peña over indigenous rights over certain lands. AGEY, Justicia, Penal, caja 88, vol. 88, exp. 34, "Causa contra el cacique de Hunucmá Pascual Chac por ocupar el y los indios del pueblo las tierras de propiedad de Juana Peña," 1856–57. For more on the Pascual Chac case and local politics in Hunucmá, see Eiss, *In the Name of El Pueblo.*

25. AGEY, PE, Comisaria Imperial, caja 225, vol. 175, exp. 52, "Solicitud de cacique de Cacalchén para que se exceptue a los vecinos de su pueblo de las faginas que les corresponden por las razones que exponen," 1864.

26. AGEY, PE, Ayuntamientos, caja 262, vol. 212, exp. 56, "Gregorio Sosa, cacique de indígenas de Chicxulub solicita al prefecto político lo exceptue del pago de contribución de sangre," 1866.

27. AGEY, Justicia, Civil, vol. 120, exp. 31, "Juicio ejecutivo de embargo al cacique Bernabé Canche por deuda a la hacienda publica," 1865.

28. AGEY, PE, Comisaria Imperial, caja 249, vol. 199, exp. 37, "Agustín Chan, cacique de Chablekal comunica al prefecto politico los abusos de autoridad cometidos por el comisario municipal de Conkal," 1866.

29. Molina's report does not mention the name of the cacique of Cenotillo. However, it is possible to deduce that this was not the incoming cacique Valentin Canché, but rather the aging Andrés Canché who had approached the defensor for succor. CAIHY, "Informe de los trabajos," 1865.

30. Ibid.

31. Ibid.

32. AGEY, PE, Empleos, caja 230, vol. 180, exp. 83, "Arturo Peón envía al prefecto superior político la terna de propuestas para cacique de Caucel," 1864.

33. CAIHY, "Informe de los trabajos," 1865.

34. Ibid.

35. Ibid.

36. Rugeley, *Rebellion Now and Forever*, 230.

37. AGEY, PE, Justicia, caja 237, vol. 187, exp. 52, "Interdicto promovido por Buenaventura Cabrera y Andrés Canché representantes de la republica de indígenas contra el Juez de Cenotillo Domingo Soberanis, Felipe Correa, y Marcos López por poblar con ganado sus fincas que afectan al pueblo" May 1865.

38. AGEY, PE, Milicia, caja; 242, vol. 192, exp; 46, "Francisco Canton comunica al comandante de la séptima división la salida de una fuerza militar con destino a Cenotillo por la invasión de los barbaros; llegada de Agustin Acereto desde la hacienda Labcheen con informes de su encuentro con los indios sublevados; invasión del pueblo de Cenotillo por los sublevados etc.," December 1865.

39. Quoted in Rugeley, *Maya Wars*, 150.

40. AGEY, PE, caja 280, vol. 230, exp. 24, "Manuel González, José Cicerol y Rafael Moreno comunican al Gobernador el informe del presidente municipal de Telchac sobre aprehensión de individuos por conspiración, alquiler de la casa de la república de indígenas, instalación del ayuntamiento, etc.," 1869.

41. AGEY, PE, Leyes y Decretos, caja 279, vol. 229, exp. 63, "Comunicado del gobernador acerca de la desaparición por decreto de las republicas de indios y solicitando informe de las existentes," 1868.

42. AGEY, PE, caja 288, vol. 238, exp. 70, "José C. comunica al gobernador la nomina de los indígenas que debieron entrar a fungir como alcaldes auxiliares en los pueblos del partido de Motul," 1869.

43. AGEY, PE, Ayuntamientos, caja 318, vol. 268, exp. 13, "Juan de Dios Col solicita al gobernador ordene al ayuntamiento no le exija cantidad de dinero que como cacique reanudo de mensuras y entrego al jefe político," 1875.

44. AGEY, Justicia, Penal, vol. 160, exp. 32, "Diligencias contra Dionicio Valencia presidente de Teablo por violaciones de garantías individuales de varios indígenas," 1872.

45. AGEY, Justicia, Penal, vol. 154, exp. 45, "Oficio del C. Gobernador del estado relativo a que los jueces de Paz 1° y 2° de Tahmek, C. C. Ignacio Gamboa y Juan Salazar, obligan a trabajos personales a varios indígenas," 1871.

Conclusion

1. AGEY, Justicia, Civil, caja 80, vol. 80, exp. 16, "Testamentarias del cacique del suburbio de Santiago, Manuel Koyoc," 1858–62.

2. AGEY, Justicia, Civil, vol. 117, exp. 6, "Diligencias practicadas en la testamentaria de indígena José de La Cruz Moo de Kopoma," 1865.

Bibliography

Archives

Archivo General de la Nación, Mexico City, Mexico
Archivo General del Estado de Yucatán, Mérida, Yucatán
Centro de Apoyo a la Investigación Histórica de Yucatán, Mérida, Yucatán

Publications

Alcalá Ferráez, Carlos. "Cólera: mortalidad y propagación en la península de Yucatán, 1833–1834," *Letras Históricas*, no. 7 (Fall 2012–Spring 2013): 115–41.

Alexander, Rani T. *Yaxcabá and the Caste War of Yucatán: An Archaeological Perspective*. Albuquerque: University of New Mexico Press, 2004.

Ancona, Eligio. *Colección de leyes, decretos, ordenes y demás disposiciones de tendencia general: expedidas por el poder legislativo del estado de Yucatan*. Mérida: Imp. de "El Eco del Comercio," 1882–89.

Andrien, Kenneth J. *Andean Worlds: Indigenous History, Culture, and Consciousness under Spanish Rule, 1532–1825 (Dialogos)*. Albuquerque: University of New Mexico Press, 2001.

Aznar Pérez, Alonso. *Colección de leyes, decretos y ordenes: o acuerdos de tendencia general, del poder legislativo del estado libre y soberano de Yucatán*. 3 vols. Mérida: Imprenta del Editor, 1849–51.

Baños Ramírez, Othón. *Liberalismo, actores y politica en Yucatán*. Mérida: Universidad Autónoma de Yucatán, 1995.

Benson, Nettie Lee. *The Provincial Deputation in Mexico: Harbinger of Provincial Autonomy, Independence, and Federalism*. Austin: University of Texas Press, 1992.

Borah, Woodrow. *Justice by Insurance: The General Indian Court of Colonial Mexico and the Legal Aides of the Half-Real*. Berkeley: University of California Press, 1983.

Bracamonte y Sosa, Pedro. *Amos y sirvientes: las haciendas de Yucatán, 1789–1860 (Tratados)*. Spanish ed. Mérida: Universidad Autónoma de Yucatán, 1993.

———. *La memoria enclaustrada: historia indígena de Yucatán, 1750–1915*. Mexico City: CIESAS, 1994.

Brading, D. A. *Miners and Merchants in Bourbon Mexico, 1763–1810*. New York: Cambridge University Press, 1971.

Brannon, Jeffrey, and Gilbert Joseph, eds. *Land, Labor, and Capital in Modern Yucatán: Essays in Regional History and Political Economy*. Tuscaloosa: University of Alabama Press, 2002.

Canclini, Nestor Garcia. *Hybrid Cultures: Strategies for Entering and Leaving Modernity*. Minneapolis: University of Minnesota Press, 2005.

Caplan, Karen. *Indigenous Citizens: Local Liberalism in Early National Oaxaca and Yucatán*. Palo Alto, Calif.: Stanford University Press, 2010.

Coronil, Fernando. "Listening to the Subaltern: The Poetics of Necolonial States." *Poetics Today* 15, no. 4 (1994): 643–58.

Craib, Raymond B. *Cartographic Mexico: A History of State Fixations and Fugitive Landscapes*. Durham, N.C.: Duke University Press, 2004.

Cutter, Charles R. *The Protector de Indios in Colonial New Mexico, 1659–1821*. Albuquerque: University of New Mexico Press, 1986.

de la Cadena, Marisol. *Indigenous Mestizos: The Politics of Race and Culture in Cuzco, Peru, 1919–1991*. Durham, N.C.: Duke University Press, 2000.

Dirks, Nicholas B., Geoff Eley, and Sherry Ortner, eds. *Culture/Power/History: A Reader in Contemporary Social Theory*. Princeton, N.J.: Princeton University Press, 1994.

Ducey, Michael T. *A Nation of Villages: Riot and Rebellion in the Mexican Huasteca, 1750–1850*. Tucson: University of Arizona Press, 2004.

Dumond, Don. *The Machete and the Cross: Campesino Rebellion in Yucatan*, Lincoln: University of Nebraska Press, 1997.

Dumond, Carol, and Don Dumond, eds. *Demography and Parish Affairs in Yucatán, 1797–1897: Documents from the Archivo de la Mitra Emeritense Selected by Joaquín de Arrigunana Peón*. Eugene: University of Oregon Press, 1982.

Dym, Jordana. *From Sovereign Villages to National States: City, State, and Federation in Central America, 1759–1839*. Albuquerque: University of New Mexico Press, 2006.

Dzul Sanchez, José Mauricio. "José Matias Quintana y las organizaciones precursoras del movimiento liberal yucateco 1812–1823." Archivo General del Estado de Yucatán. www.archivogeneral.yucatan.gob.mx/Bicentenario/JMQ%20Organizacion%20precursoras%20yucatecas.htm.

Eiss, Paul K. *In the Name of El Pueblo: Place, Community, and the Politics of History in Yucatán*. Durham, N.C.: Duke University Press, 2010.

Farriss, Nancy Marguerite. *Maya Society under Colonial Rule: The Collective Enterprise of Survival*. Princeton, N.J.: Princeton University Press, 1984.

Friedrich, Paul. "The Legitimacy of a *Cacique*." In Steffin Schmidt et al., eds., *Friends, Followers and Factions: A Reader in Political Clientelism*. Los Angeles: University of California Press, 1977.

Gabbert, Wolfgang. *Becoming Maya: Ethnicity and Social Inequality in Yucatán since 1500*. Tucson: University of Arizona Press, 2004.

García, Melchor Campos. "Faccionalismo y votaciones en Yucatán, 1824–1832." *Historia Mexicana* 51, no. 1 (2001): 59–102.

———. *Las constituciones históricas de Yucatán, 1824–1905*. Mérida: Universidad Autónoma de Yucatán, 2009.

———, ed. *Republicanismos emergentes: continuidades y rupturas en Yucatán y Puebla, 1786–1869*. Mérida: Universidad Autónoma de Yucatán, 2010.

Gibson, Charles. *The Aztecs under Spanish Rule: A History of the Indians of the Valley of Mexico, 1519–1810*. Stanford, Calif.: Stanford University Press, 1964.

Grandin, Greg. *The Blood of Guatemala: A History of Race and Nation*. Durham, N.C.: Duke University Press, 2000.

Guardino, Peter. *The Time of Liberty: Popular Political Culture in Oaxaca, 1750–1850*. Durham, N.C.: Duke University Press, 2005.

Güémez Pineda, Arturo. "Everyday Forms of Maya Rustling." In Jeffrey Brannon and Gilbert Joseph, eds., *Land, Labor, and Capital in Modern Yucatán: Essays in Regional History and Political Economy*. Tuscaloosa: University of Alabama Press, 2002.

———. *Liberalismo en tierras del caminante: Yucatán, 1812–1840*. Spanish ed. Michoacán: Colegio de Michoacán, 1994.

———. *Mayas, gobierno y tierras frente a la acometida liberal en Yucatán, 1812–1847*. Spanish ed. Mérida: Universidad Autónoma de Yucatán, 2005.

———. "Municipalización y guerra de castas: testimonios de la restricción a la libertad civil maya en Yucatán, 1847–1869." In Melchor Campos García, *Republicanismos emergentes: continuidades y rupturas en Yucatán y Puebla, 1786–1869*. Mérida: Universidad Autónoma de Yucatán, 2010.

Guha, Ranajit. "The Prose of Counter-Insurgency." In Nicholas Dirks et al., eds., *Culture/Power/History: A Reader in Contemporary Social Theory*. Princeton, N.J.: Princeton University Press, 1994.

Gupta, Akhil. "Blurred Boundaries: The Discourse of Corruption, the Culture of Politics, and the Imagined State." In Aradhana Sharma and Akhil Gupta, eds., *The Anthropology of the State: A Reader*. Hoboken, N.J.: Wiley-Blackwell, 2006.

Hall, Frederic. *Invasion of Mexico by the French; And the Reign of Maximilian I; with a Sketch of the Empress Carlota*. New York: James Miller, 1868.

Haskett, Robert S. "Living in Two Worlds: Cultural Continuity and Change among Cuernavaca's Colonial Indigenous Ruling Elite." *Ethnohistory* 35, no. 1 (1988): 34–59.

Haslip, Joan. *The Crown of Mexico: Maximilian and His Empress Carlota*. New York: Avon Books, 1973.

Herzog, Tamar. *Defining Nations: Immigrants and Citizens in Early Modern Spain and Spanish America.* New Haven, Conn.: Yale University Press, 2011.

Hu-Dehart, Evelyn. *Yaqui Resistance and Survival: The Struggle for Land and Autonomy, 1821–1910.* Madison: University of Wisconsin Press, 1984.

Joseph, Gilbert, and Daniel Nugent, eds. *Everyday Forms of State Formation: Revolution and the Negotiation of Rule in Modern Mexico.* Durham, N.C.: Duke University Press, 1994.

Katz, Friedrich. "Labor Conditions on Haciendas in Porfirian Mexico: Some Trends and Tendencies." *Hispanic American Historical Review* 54, no. 1 (1974): 1–47.

———, ed. *Riot, Rebellion, and Revolution: Rural Social Conflict in Mexico.* Princeton, N.J.: Princeton University Press, 1988.

Kellogg, Susan. *Law and the Transformation of Aztec Society, 1500–1700.* Norman: University of Oklahoma Press, 1995.

Larson, Brooke. *Trials of Nation Making: Liberalism, Race, and Ethnicity in the Andes, 1810–1910.* Cambridge: Cambridge University Press, 2004.

Lentz, Mark. "Assassination in Yucatán: Crime and Society, 1792–1812." Ph.D. diss., Tulane University, 2009. ProQuest (UMI: 3375155).

Lira, Andrés. *Comunidades indígenas en frente a la ciudad de Mexico.* Zamora: Colegio de Michoacan, 1983.

Lockhart, James. *Men of Cajamarca: Social and Biographical Study of the First Conquerors of Peru.* Austin: University of Texas Press, 1972.

Lockhart, James, and Stuart Schwartz. *Early Latin America: A History of Colonial Spanish America and Brazil.* New York: Cambridge University Press, 1983.

Mallon, Florencia E. *Courage Tastes of Blood: The Mapuche Community of Nicolás Ailío and the Chilean State, 1906–2001.* Durham, N.C.: Duke University Press, 2005.

McCrea, Heather. *Diseased Relations: Epidemics, Public Health, and State-Building in Yucatán, Mexico, 1847–1924.* Albuquerque: University of New Mexico Press, 2011.

McNamara, Patrick J. *Sons of the Sierra: Juárez, Díaz, and the People of Ixtlán, Oaxaca, 1855–1920.* Chapel Hill: University of North Carolina Press, 2007.

Metcalf, Alida C. *Go-betweens and the Colonization of Brazil, 1500–1600.* Austin: University of Texas Press, 2005.

Meyer, Michael, William Sherman, and Susan Deeds. *The Course of Mexican History.* New York: Oxford University Press, 2010.

Mitchell, Timothy. "Society, Economy, and the State Effect." In Aradhana Sharma and Akhil Gupta, eds., *The Anthropology of the State: A Reader.* Hoboken, N.J.: Wiley-Blackwell, 2006.

Patch, Robert. *Maya and Spaniard in Yucatán, 1648–1812.* Palo Alto, Calif.: Stanford University Press, 1994.

Polushin, Michael. "Bureaucratic Conquest, Bureaucratic Culture: Town and Office in Chiapas, 1780–1832." Ph.D. diss., Tulane University, 1999. ProQuest (UMI: 9971275).

Quezada, Sergio. *Breve historia de Yucatán.* Mexico D.F.: Colegio de Mexico, 2001.

———. *Maya Lords and Lordship: The Formation of Colonial Society in Yucatán, 1350–1600.* Norman: University of Oklahoma Press, 2014.

———. *Pueblos y caciques yucatecos, 1550–1580.* Spanish ed. Mexico City: El Colegio de México, 1993.

Quintal Martín, Fidelio. "Inicio interpretativo de la correspondencia en maya sobre la 'guerra de castas' (1842–1866)." *Revista de la Universidad Autónoma de Yucatán,* no. 3 (1988): 3–19.

Rappaport, Joanne. *Cumbe Reborn: An Andean Ethnography of History.* Chicago: University of Chicago Press, 1990.

Reed, Nelson. *The Caste War of Yucatán.* Stanford, Calif.: Stanford University Press, 2001.

Restall, Matthew. *Maya Conquistador.* Boston: Beacon Press, 1998.

———. *The Maya World: Yucatec Culture and Society, 1550–1850.* Palo Alto, Calif.: Stanford University Press, 1997.

———. *2012 and the End of the World: The Western Roots of the Maya Apocalypse.* Lanham, Md.: Rowman and Littlefield, 2011.

Richmond, Douglas. *Conflict and Carnage in Yucatán: Liberals, the Second Empire, and Maya Revolutionaries, 1855–1876.* Tuscaloosa: University of Alabama Press, 2015.

Rivero, Piedad Peniche. *La historia secreta de la hacienda henequenera de Yucatán: deudas, migración y resistencia maya (1879–1915).* Mérida: Instituto de Cultura de Yucatán, 2010.

Roys, Ralph L. *The Titles of Ebtun.* Brooklyn: AMS Press, 1983.

Rugeley, Terry. "From Santa Iglesia to Santa Cruz: Yucatecan Popular Religion in Peace and War, 1800–1876." In Edward Terry et al., eds., *Peripheral Visions: Politics, Society and the Challenges of Modernity in Yucatán.* Tuscaloosa: University of Alabama Press, 2010.

———. *Maya Wars: Ethnographic Accounts from Nineteenth-Century Yucatán.* Norman: University of Oklahoma Press, 2001.

———. *Of Wonders and Wise Men: Religion and Popular Culture in Southeast Mexico, 1800–1876.* Austin: University of Texas Press, 2001.

———. *Rebellion Now and Forever: Mayas, Hispanics, and Caste War Violence in Yucatán, 1800–1880.* Palo Alto, Calif.: Stanford University Press, 2009.

———. "Rural Political Violence and the Origins of the Caste War." *The Americas* 53, no. 4 (1997): 469–96.

———. *Yucatán's Maya Peasantry and the Origins of the Caste War.* Austin: University of Texas Press, 1996.

Scott, James C. *Weapons of the Weak: Everyday Forms of Peasant Resistance.* New Haven, Conn.: Yale University Press, 1987.

Schmidt, Steffen, James C. Scott, Carl Lande, and Laura Guasti, eds. *Friends, Followers and Factions: A Reader in Political Clientelism.* Los Angeles: University of California Press, 1977.

Sharma, Aradhana, and Akhil Gupta, eds. *The Anthropology of the State: A Reader.* Hoboken, N.J.: Wiley-Blackwell, 2006.

Solís, Juan Francisco Molina. *Historia de Yucatán desde la independencia hasta la época actual.* vol. 2. Mérida: Cia Tipografica Yucateca, 1927.

Stephens, John Lloyd. *Incidents of Travel in Yucatán*, Vol. 1. New York: Harper and Brothers, 1843.

Tapia, Carlos. *La organización politica indígena en el Yucatán independiente.* Mérida: Universidad Autónoma de Yucatán, 1985.

Terry, Edward, Gilbert Joseph, Edward Moseley, and Ben Fallaw, eds. *Peripheral Visions: Politics, Society and the Challenges of Modernity in Yucatán.* Tuscaloosa: University of Alabama Press, 2010.

Thompson, Philip C. *Tekantó, a Maya Town in Colonial Yucatán.* New Orleans, La.: Tulane University Middle American Research Institute, 2000.

Thomson, Sinclair. *We Alone Will Rule: Native Andean Politics in the Age of Insurgency.* Madison: University of Wisconsin Press, 2003.

Thurner, Mark. *From Two Republics to One Divided: Contradictions of Postcolonial Nationmaking in Andean Peru.* Durham. N.C.: Duke University Press, 1997.

Vázquez de Knauth, Josefina. *Nacionalismo y educación en México.* Mexico City: El Colegio de México, 1970.

Walker, Charles F. *Smoldering Ashes: Cuzco and the Creation of Republican Peru, 1780–1840.* Durham, N.C.: Duke University Press, 1999.

Wells, Allen. *Yucatán's Gilded Age: Haciendas, Henequen, and International Harvester, 1860–1915.* Albuquerque: University of New Mexico Press, 1985.

Wells, Allen, and Gilbert Joseph. *Summer of Discontent, Seasons of Upheaval: Elite Politics and Rural Insurgency in Yucatán, 1876–1915.* Palo Alto, Calif.: Stanford University Press, 1996.

Wolf, Eric R. "Aspects of Group Relations in a Complex Society: Mexico." *American Anthropologist* 58, no. 6 (1956): 1065–78.

Yannakakis, Yanna. *The Art of Being In-between: Native Intermediaries, Indian Identity, and Local Rule in Colonial Oaxaca.* Durham, N.C.: Duke University Press, 2008.

Yashar, Deborah J. *Contesting Citizenship in Latin America: The Rise of Indigenous Movements and the Postliberal Challenge.* Cambridge: Cambridge University Press, 2005.

Young, Eric Van. *The Other Rebellion: Popular Violence, Ideology, and the Mexican Struggle for Independence, 1810–1821.* Palo Alto, Calif.: Stanford University Press, 2002.

Zuleta, María, ed. *La diputación provincial de Yucatán: actas de sesiones, 1813–1814, 1820–1821.* Mexico City: Instituto de Investigaciones Dr. José María Luis Mora, 2006.

Index

Page numbers in italic type refer to maps.